THIRD EDITION

PRISONERS' GUERRILLA HANDBOOK

TO CORRESPONDENCE PROGRAMS
IN THE UNITED STATES & CANADA

BY **JON MARC TAYLOR**, PhD

Edited by Susan Schwartzkopf, MA

Forward by Rev. Vivian Nixon

HIGH SCHOOL • VOCATIONAL • PARALEGAL
LAW • COLLEGE • GRADUATE COURSES

PRISON LEGAL NEWS
BRATTLEBORO, VERMONT • SEATTLE, WASHINGTON

Dedicated to Protecting Human Rights

Copyright © 2009 by Prison Legal News.

Prison Legal News is a project of the Human Rights Defense Center.

ISBN 978-0-9819385-0-9

All rights reserved. No part of this publication may be reproduced or transmitted in any form or by any means, electronic or mechanical, including photocopying, recording, or any information storage or retrieval system, without permission in writing from the publisher.

Prison Legal News
2400 NW 80th Street, PMB #148
Seattle, WA 98117
206-246-1022
www.prisonlegalnews.org

The Prisoner's Guerrilla Handbook to Correspondence Programs in the United States and Canada, 3rd edition, by Jon Marc Taylor, edited by Susan Schwartzkopf.

Typography and design by Jules Siegel

Cover illustration by Jules Siegel based on a photograph by Ryan Brenizer

Set in Hypatia Sans

Contents

Publisher's Introduction 5

Foreword 7

About the Author 10

The Need for this Book 14

How to Use this Book 17
- How to Use the Outlines as an Evaluation Tool 17
- Summation 24

Factors in Selecting a Program 25

Accreditation 27

Diploma Mills 30

The Least Expensive Path to a Baccalaureate 32

Other College-Level Credit Sources 36

Managing Your Education 42
- How Independent Learning Works 47
- Words to the Wise 48
- Study Tips 48
- Anti-Procrastination Tips 49
- The Highly Productive Learner 49
- Create Your Own University 51

High School Outlines 55

Vocational Program Outlines 73

Paralegal Program Outlines 121

Undergraduate Programs (Colleges & Universities) 136

Graduate Program Outlines 199

Index 215

Publisher's Introduction

By Paul Wright
Editor and Co-Founder
Prison Legal News

The third edition of the *Prisoners' Guerrilla Handbook to Correspondence Programs in the United States and Canada* is the first book title to be printed and published by Prison Legal News.

For a number of years I had considered the idea of publishing books, especially non-fiction reference and research books that would be useful to prisoners but that commercial publishers were unlikely to publish due to the perception of a limited (and unprofitable) market. When I discussed this with PLN's staff a few years ago everyone thought it was a good idea but we lacked the resources to pursue it. So the project was shelved.

Then in early 2007 Julie Zimmerman, owner of Biddle Publishing, called and told me she was retiring and asked if PLN would be interested in taking over the printing and distribution of *Prisoners' Guerrilla Handbook to Correspondence Programs in the United States and Canada*. We had been distributing the book for several years; it had been a good seller and fulfilled an important need for prisoners seeking to further their educations while in prison. We had recently hired PLN's advertising and outreach director, Susan Schwartzkopf, and she came to PLN with a Master's degree in teaching and 12 years experience instructing adult immigrants in English. She was enthusiastic about the project. We decided that rather than just reprint the book we would update it with current information and also professionalize its look and appearance over prior editions.

You are now holding the final product in your hands. It has been a learning experience, but we learned how to publish and distribute a national magazine, and thus we can learn how to publish and distribute books as well. Jon and Susan have put a tremendous amount of work

We aim to publish high quality non-fiction, reference and research books that are of particular interest to prisoners.

We decided to update the book with current information and also professionalize its look and appearance.

into this updated edition and it shows in the results. Jules Siegel did a great job on the book cover and the layout and presentation. We are very proud to have *Prisoners' Guerrilla Handbook to Correspondence Programs In the United States and Canada*, 3rd edition, as the first book in the Prison Legal News publishing line. We aim to publish high quality non-fiction, reference and research books that are of particular interest to prisoners. For authors seeking a publisher we have a very simple formula based on my own experiences with the book publishing industry: a simple, easy to understand book contract that ensures the author gets a very competitive royalty on every book sold. We think it is possible to publish high quality books while still adequately compensating writers. Hopefully we are correct.

As *Prison Legal News* approaches it's 20th year of magazine publishing, with the top ranked prison-related news website in the world, bringing our readers non-fiction, reference and research books they can use to make a positive difference in their lives—before, during and after a stint in jail or prison—this seems like the natural thing to do.

Foreword

> This book demystifies the idea of getting a post secondary education while incarcerated.

By Vivian Nixon

I CAN ONLY IMAGINE how different my life would have been if I had had access to the information contained in this book during the three and a half years I spent in a New York State prison. I spent much of 1998-2001 without any meaningful educational development, career counseling, or help in choosing a direction for my future. During that time, college was available at one female correctional facility in the state of New York; however, it was a maximum-security facility, and because I was medium security status, I was barred from that opportunity. I assumed that there was no other way I could go to college. Too many incarcerated women and men make similar assumptions. This book demystifies the idea of getting a post secondary education while incarcerated. It provides concrete information and practical solutions to people who have few resources and support systems at their disposal.

The value of providing higher education opportunities to people in prison cannot be overstated. You are reading this guide because either you are in prison seeking ways to obtain a higher education, or you care about people in prison who want to get an education. For many of us, education has been the primary means of overcoming the stigma of incarceration, but more than that, it has enlightened us and given us opportunities to engage in the public debate about policies that seem antithetical to the goals of civil society.

One such debate continues to ensue around systemic restoration of higher education programs in America's prisons. Whether it be through the restoration of Pell Grant eligibility or by some other means, there is no shortage of opinions when it comes to the discussion of what many insist on calling "correctional education". The divergence of opinions often begins with the basic question of whether education should be the responsibility of correctional facilities at all. Certainly if the need for basic education inside of correctional facilities is still in question, post

> **The educational needs of incarcerated people are as diverse as the educational needs of people in free society.**

With every year of education, the risk of criminal recidivism declines.

secondary education has its own set of debates. Who should pay for it? Should it consist primarily of technical and vocational certificates or associate and bachelor's degrees? Is it right to offer college to people in prison when people on the outside are struggling for access to higher education?

These questions dominated much of the discussion at a recent forum on correctional education held at the Prisoner Reentry Institute of John Jay College of Criminal Justice. As I sat at the roundtable mentally preparing to respond to these questions, I wondered why it was up to any of us to decide what type of education was appropriate for people in prison as if they were a monolithic population. Indeed, my experience has been, and all of you who will take advantage of the information in this handbook know, that the educational needs of incarcerated people are as diverse as the educational needs of people in free society. Furthermore, my understanding of a great society is one that has a moral imperative to provide all its citizens (including those who are incarcerated) with the opportunity and the means to attain education. Not everyone at the roundtable adopted the progressive ideas about which I talked steadfastly throughout the two-day event.

To understand the logic behind such passionate talk, one must understand not only where I have been, but also what I do. Through the College and Community Fellowship (CCF), for the past seven years I have worked with an incredible group of students who illustrate the value of educational opportunity. CCF—the first organization in New York State to offer higher education support to formerly incarcerated women as a primary strategy for helping them rebuild their lives—is charitably housed at the Graduate Center, The City University of New York. Our internal data confirm what other studies have shown: with every year of education, the risk of criminal recidivism declines. Yet higher education opportunities for people in prison and people with criminal convictions are severely limited.

College programs in prisons were funded through federal Pell Grants from the 1970s through 1994. In the 1990's higher education in prison was attacked and Congress passed the 1993 crime bill, which included a provision that made prisoners ineligible for federal student financial aid. This was reinforced by the reauthorization of the Higher Education Act in 1994, and most college programs in prisons closed their doors. In addition, Congress limited access to Pell Grants for students outside of prison based on certain felony convictions. Since then, numerous studies have shown that college in prison programs reduce recidivism rates, reduce violence and disciplinary incidents in prisons, encourage the children of incarcerated parents to pursue education, and create a general sense of hope among incarcerated individuals.

There has been tremendous pushback against efforts to reinstate public support for college in prison. A few privately funded programs do operate across the country; however, the focus in the past 10 years has shifted to what happens to people when they are released from prison. The chance of deep social reintegration for people leaving prison is supported by the completion of higher education degrees. The individual and public benefits of education are too many to list here and are well known. Briefly, we know that higher education increases employability, reduces recidivism, and has a positive correlation with good health, overall quality of life, and deep social integration. Public benefits include increased tax revenues, greater workplace productivity, increased consumption, increased workforce flexibility, and decreased reliance on government financial support.

This book will help you get solid answers to important questions about the possibility of obtaining an education while in an environment where access is limited. The book presents well-organized and accurate information about hundreds of accredited schools from which you may choose the program most appropriate for your needs. You deserve an education, despite your status of incarceration. To the extent that this book makes the possibility of education a step closer to reality, it is a tool for social justice.

I believe that in a country where second chances and opportunity are professed values, democratic access to high-quality higher education must include access for people in prison. We cannot bar the most vulnerable people from the very thing that has the greatest potential to change their lives and defend our image as the world's model for equality, justice, and democracy.

A tool of social justice

About the Author

> I have spent more than half—and all of my adult—life behind bars, some 28 years and counting.

As of this writing, I have spent more than half—and all of my adult—life behind bars, some 28 years and counting. Since 1982, I have been enrolled in some form of Post-Secondary Correctional Education (PSCE). Initially matriculating in Ball State University's extension program at the Indiana State Reformatory (since then renamed the Pendleton Correctional Center), and as a naive freshman, I struggled to make sense of my first three college courses of introductory anthropology, composition, and political science. By the end of the quarter, besides making the Dean's List, I was hooked on the legal high of expanding my mind in a way the "man" could not stop or ever take away. In 1984, I received my Associate of Arts Degree, and in 1988 I earned my Bachelor of Science, cum laude, majoring in History with enough hours for minors in English and Political Science. By commencement, I had been admitted to the Golden Key national honor society, as well as the international honor societies of Pi Gamma Mu (social sciences) and Phi Alpha Theta (history).

Through the encouragement and good offices of my mentor, Dr. Ross H. Van Ness, we were able to put together a program of graduate study. It was an administrative and bureaucratic ordeal that eventually involved the intercessions of the Dean of Continuing Education and Corrections Commissioner, among many procedural dramas. In 1990, I was the first prisoner in the history of Indiana to earn a graduate degree. Specifically, my accomplishment was a Master of Arts in Executive Development for Public Service, with a major in Adult and Community Education. Acting on the suggestion of Dr. Van Ness, I applied to and became the first maximum security prisoner in the country to be accepted to an accredited American university's doctoral program in adult and community education. Unable to meet the degree's residency requirements, after one semester of study I was forced to curtail, though not abandon, my quest for a doctorate degree. Addicted to the endless possibilities of higher education, I regrouped and made the best of my circumstances, continuing my enrollment in other courses. In 1992, I received a graduate certificate in Military History, concurrently beginning work on a second baccalaureate in criminal justice and psychology.

After thirteen years in Indiana, and a sentence reduction significantly influenced by my educational achievements, I was transferred to Missouri to begin a consecutive sentence. Continuing to pursue my education, I enrolled in Washington State University's Bachelor of Arts program, but half way through, due to the foreign language requirement, I decided to shift programs. Transferring the hours earned at WSU to the University of Alabama, I completed the Certificate in Criminal Justice studies. (Sadly this is an opportunity no longer available via correspondence study.)

After a lot of searching for a viable program and a year of applying for and negotiating with the Department of Corrections and Kennedy-Western University, I was admitted to the school's doctoral program in public administration. Two more years of course by course completions including the arduous and highly creative researching and writing of my dissertation ("PELL GRANTS FOR PRISONERS: An Issue in Public Administration") resulted in the conferment of a PhD in 2004. Not the academic field I initiated as my doctoral goal, but one that was viable at the time considering the circumstances. My quest, however, for a doctorate in education is still a dream I retain, and one day, I hope I will become "doctor-doctor Taylor." For the past few years, I have been working on a graduate certificate from Louisiana State University in the Foundations of Non-Profit Administration. This is an example of yet another traditional correspondence program that has also been eliminated.

After two and a half decades of continuing education, attending and/or taking courses from half a dozen American universities and one from Queen's College in England, my correctional education experience extends beyond these not so humble credits. While enrolled in Ball State's program, I served as a volunteer special programs clerk processing financial aid applications, coalescing enrollment packages, coordinating textbook distributions, advising curriculum, and providing service support in a plethora of situations. Since my transfer from that special program, I have been solely responsible for all aspects of my furthered education. Much has been learned between the differences of theory taught, and experience earned. This book is the progeny of my academic expeditions.

Besides the accumulation of academic credentials, I have utilized the communication skills and abilities I gained from a liberal arts education to analyze and reason to try to comprehend why Post-Secondary

> "I am only an average man, but, by George, I work harder than the average man."
>
> — THEODORE ROOSEVELT

> "I would rather have a mind opened by wonder than one closed by belief."
> —Gerry Spence

Correctional Education has so positively influenced my own life as well as countless others. Beginning in 1989, with the publication of my first article in the Canadian-based *Journal of Prisoners on Prisons* (which I now serve on the editorial board), I have researched and written about PSCE in particular and the criminal justice system in general. My work has been widely disseminated, reaching specialized as well as broad spectrum audiences. In the prison press, such publications as *The Angolite, The Chainlink Chronicle, Fortune News, Inside Journal, Justicia, Prison Legal News, The Prison Mirror* (the oldest continuously published prison paper in the nation), *Southland Prison News*, and the *Straight Low* have all published my work. My op-ed pieces have been run by major newspapers, such as the *New York Times*, the *Indianapolis Star*, the *St. Louis Post-Dispatch*, as well as a dozen others. Magazines printing my writings have been in *Business Week, The Nation, Prison Life*, and *The World & I*. Specialized criminal justice publications have also printed my peer-reviewed papers in such journals as *Corrections & Higher Education Monograph, Criminal Justice, Educational Policy, Journal of Contemporary Criminal Justice*, and *The Journal of Correctional Education*. And my original and published works have been included in the anthologies of *America's Prisons: Opposing Viewpoints, Doing Time, Higher Education in Prison: A Contradiction of Terms?* and *Turnstile Justice: Issues in American Corrections*.

Beyond publications, some of my writings have been honored by academic and journalistic associations. Of that work, academic treatises have received First Place and Runner-Up recognition in the student essay contest of the section on Criminal Justice Administration of the American Society for Public Administration. Reporting on the issue of Pell Grants for prisoners, my series first received The Nation/I.F. Stone Student Journalism Award. And on the same spring evening, while Dr. Van Ness was in Valparaiso, Indiana, accepting my Outstanding Adult Learner Award in that state, my mother was attending the Robert F. Kennedy Journalism Awards in Washington, DC, receiving my first place student journalism award for "Pell Grants for Prisoners?" Moreover, my *New York Times* op-ed piece was read into the United States Congressional Record by Senator Paul Simon.

Benefiting from my knowledge, I wrote a policy paper, "Calling for Sheepskins," that advocated the allocation of the rebate funds (several million dollars annually) from the Inmate Collect Calling Phone System-MCI contract to refinance PSCE in Missouri prisons. These had been discontinued after the loss of prisoners' Pell Grant eligibility. Publishing the piece in the *Cry Justice Journal*, and drawing upon experience gained in the Pell Grant fight, a grassroots lobbying campaign was initiated. The results of those continuing efforts was the introduction for three consecutive General Assembly sessions of the Missouri Legislature of legislation to achieve the goal of reinstituting fully-funded Post-Secondary Correctional Education opportunities in the state's penal system. Sadly, while being approved by committee, the legislation was never passed by the full assembly, and the rebate portion of the telephone contract was later eliminated. Ways are still being sought to return on-site college programs to the nation's prisons.

My qualifications summarized

In summation, there are few others more qualified than I to compose this guide. My credentials are presented not in vain hubris, but in the well-worn knowledge that any efforts attempted, much less achieved, by a prisoner are routinely subjected by the larger world to discredit them. If there are others more able and involved to support this marketing niche, then please let them come forth and educate us all. With the experience of the first two editions of this guide, this third edition continues to define the data and hopefully expand the utility of the overall presentation. Your continuing contributions of comments, criticisms, questions, and success stories (some of which are chronicled in the following pages) are valued for their insights and inspirations. Please continue to share them with me, adding to my education and improving the opportunities for us all.

> **Drawing upon experience gained in the Pell Grant's fight, a grassroots lobbying campaign was initiated.**

The Need for this Book

For the majority of American prisoners, the only way to take college courses and earn degrees is via correspondence study at their own expense.

S ETTING FORTH my bona fides, the need for this book has progressively grown apparent over the years of my incarceration in the prison-industrial complex, and even more so since the first edition a decade ago. With the elimination of prisoners' Pell Grant eligibility, half of the onsite PSCE programs across the nation have closed their doors, and of those remaining, half again have condensed their curriculum offerings and/or reduced their enrollments. A follow-up survey by my co-researchers Dr. Richard Tewksbury and graduate assistant David Erickson, of the University of Louisville, revealed continued erosion of programs, curriculums, and enrollments years after the expulsion of prisoners from the Pell Grant program. The latest example of this continuing trend is Utah State University's closure of the penal system's bachelor and master degrees program in 2007.

Thankfully, some states, like Indiana and Texas, and/or schools, like Patten University in Oakland, California and the University of North Carolina, provide or create a new means for prisoner-students to continue their post-secondary educations. If you find yourself incarcerated with these or similar opportunities, consider yourself fortunate and take full advantage of them. For the majority of American prisoners, however, the only way to take college courses and earn degrees is to do so via correspondence study at their own expense. For over a decade, I have been taking various correspondence classes from an assortment of universities, comparing and contrasting them to classroom instruction, and have learned some important lessons along the way. Continually I encourage and advise my fellow prisoners on how to select a program, maneuver through the myriad of bureaucratic obstacles, successfully complete course work and eventually earn a degree. I realize continuously the need for a guide specifically designed for prisoner-students to assist them through all the many tasks they will have to accomplish to be successful students.

"Make big plans, aim high in hope and work."
— DANIEL H. BURNHAM

There are other general correspondence guides available on the market, such as Petersen's *Independent Study Catalog and Distance Learning Programs*, Thorsen's *Guide to Campus-Free College Degrees*, the pamphlets *The Home-Based College and Education Programs Catalog*, as well as PEN American Center's (free) *Prison Education Opportunities* guides. These are good general references to college-level correspondence programs, and have been reviewed in preparation for this edition. None of these, however, go beyond basic program listings or focus on the unique needs and restrictions of the prisoner-student, and they rarely report on vocational and paralegal correspondence opportunities. As Glenn MacDonald from a prison in Delaware comments, "I had purchased *College Degrees By Mail* and was disappointed, as it was really for those in the 'free world'." Others, like Regents College's "List of External Graduate Programs," are no longer published.

Moreover, some distance education programs listed in the guides mentioned above do not permit prisoner enrollments. Reasons for these student exclusions vary. Some are structural limitations, such as varying residency and tutorial requirements, at programs such as Antioch University, Johnson State College, and Oak Brook College of Law. Other schools, like Johnson Bible College, Southwestern Assemblies of God University and Judson College, however, claim they are "not staffed and equipped to meet the correspondence needs of inmates" or require former prisoners to "establish themselves in a community and be involved in a church for no less than one year" or do not admit "any program persons who are incarcerated or who are otherwise restricted in their movements."

Experimental Internet prison education

Then there is the proliferation of "on-line" or "Internet-delivered" or "web-based" course and degree offerings. Some guides report solely on these distance education opportunities. Other than an exciting experimental program in Maryland created by the writer of the foreword to the second edition, Dr. Alice Tracy, and a reference to a firewall-restricted program in Arizona, I do not know of a single prison that permits its prisoners Internet access that would allow open access to on-line college programs. Thus, of the approximately 2,500 online schools with three and a half million student enrollments, none are of any use to prisoners. What is more problematic, though, are those distance education opportunities

Only one prison allows open access to on-line college programs.

One unique feature of this edition is the elimination of schools that educate solely via the Internet.

that are exclusively delivered via the Internet. When preparing the second edition, the University of Maryland and University of Massachusetts, both excellent schools with prolific distance education offerings, had to be dropped from the listings because they had gone exclusively on-line. Without Internet access, these programs might as well not exist for prisoner-students. In the second edition 20 schools that were profiled in the first edition are now online only programs. The third edition now has 40 programs, including the excellent Penn State Distance Education School, that are no longer available to prisoner-students.

For this reason, one feature unique to the *Prisoners' Guerrilla Handbook* is the elimination of schools who educate solely via the Internet, and the editing of all known on-line course listings. This is just another example of how the PGH is written from the perspective of the inside out.

By referring to this guide, you the reader have affirmed the need for it. I sincerely hope it is helpful in your quest for furthering your education, expanding your horizons, and enlightening the limitless potential within yourself. Your letters of how you completed a course, got your degree, used portions of this book to educate and encourage others, and how you are using your abilities and acquired educations to make the world a better place all inspire me. If it wasn't for your repeated entreaties to update PGH yet again, I wouldn't be back at this maddening, frustrating and awe-inspiring grind. Thank you all for giving continuing purpose to my life and skills.

> **"If you would plant for days, plant flowers.**
> **If you would plant for years, plant trees.**
> **If you would plant for eternity, plant ideas."**
>
> —Proverb

How to Use this Book

The purpose of this book is to help you to focus your choices while presenting as many options as possible in search for correspondence programs that fulfill your goals.

Once you have determined what it is that you want to accomplish a whole set of criteria can be used to narrow your choices. The program outlines in this handbook are designed to help you clearly understand your choices and fulfill the criteria you determine as the best ones to meet your personal needs.

Each of the five section outline designs of this handbook share a similar structure, while having some unique features that best present the information describing what they offer. By applying your personal criteria you can quickly compare programs, selecting those that initially appear to meet your needs. These program profiles, however, are just that: profiles. Once you have identified the programs that are of interest you need to write for their brochures, catalogs, and application/enrollment forms. Since the material is free, write as many programs that look attractive to you. All it costs is a stamp.

Each of the five section outline designs of this handbook share a similar structure, while having some unique features.

How to Use the Outlines as an Evaluation Tool

HIGH SCHOOL

CATALOG INFO	Lets you know how current the materials are from which the outlines are based.
ACCREDITATION	Which agencies and associations accredit the program. SEE: the section on ACCREDITATION further on in this guide for a detailed description of importance of, criteria for, and listing of reliable accreditation associations.

DIPLOMA Whether or not the program offers a diploma and the number of Carnegie Units (the standard high school-level credit measurement unit, with a semester-term class usually equivalent to a one-half Carnegie Unit) needed to meet the diploma's graduation requirements.

CO-CREDITS Whether or not some or all of the courses available can be taken for college-level co-credit as well. This option allows a student to fulfill diploma requirements, while very inexpensively completing a number of college credits, thus reducing the cost of a degree sometime in the future.

TUITION Probably the most important criteria to the prisoner-student. Tuition cost is broken down, where the program's materials allow, to the expense of a standard one-half Carnegie Unit. This allows easy cost comparison between programs. ER (Effective Rate) is the formula computing all of a school's added-on per course fees beyond the listed tuition cost, thus providing the real cost per unit. ER's are the figures you should use when comparing and contrasting various programs' per unit costs. Cheaper is not necessarily better, but with all other criteria (especially accreditation) being equal, I would go with the less expensive program.

TEXT COSTS The most common fluctuating cost between programs due to the books and materials assigned to a particular course. This criteria provides a range from the lowest cost of books for a course to the highest cost for a particular class. More common in the third edition is the average (AVG) cost of texts per course. You will have to write for the program's catalog for specific text costs, but not all schools' materials provide this information. You may have to write for a particular course's bibliography and costs. Many schools offer the opportunity to purchase used texts. I have always chosen this option to save money (approximately two-thirds the cost of a new text), and have never been shortchanged on the materials needed for a course.

TIME LIMITS Lets you know the maximum period you have to complete a course, and where provided the minimum time in which a course can be completed. Remember that these time limits include mailing time, professor evaluation, and return shipping. Common practice is to permit only two lesson submissions at a time; though, other arrangements can sometimes be negotiated. So factor in these time elements in your scheduling. Additionally, if the program offers time extensions, the number of, length, and fees for such are noted. Based upon personal experience, the shortest period of time I ever completed a class from enrollment to final exam, was five months and one week. The majority of this time was spent waiting for lesson submissions to be evaluated and returned. I would be hesitant to enroll in a program that does not allow a minimum of nine months for course completion before an extension period needs to be purchased if necessary.

TRANSFER HOURS Provides you with information if previously earned school credits can be applied to the diploma program, thus reducing your cost and time in fulfilling the number of necessary units to graduate. And if provided in the program's materials, also includes the number of units you are allowed to transfer, or conversely the number of units you must take from the program to graduate. The acceptance of transfer units is wholly at the discretion of the receiving program, and usually is based on the units being from an accredited program and the accepting school having a similarly related course. Finally, if the school being outlined does not offer a diploma program, there is no need to transfer units to it, and this criteria is simply then noted as: "Non-Applicable."

COURSES This lets you know the category and number in each category of the classes offered by the program. For a more detailed description of the individual courses, write to the schools for their catalogs.

COMMENTS This criteria provides an evaluation of the tuition rates and other relevant information that might be of interest to the prisoner-student. Extensive offerings, usually a course category of ten or more classes, is noted for quick reference. Also unique offerings can be noted here. If incarcerated students are enrolled this is cited because it advises you that the school has at least some administrative experience in dealing with the unique situation of prisoner-student study.

VOCATIONAL PROGRAMS

PROGRAM The title or category of the offering outlined.

FOUNDED Provides you with a reference to the longevity and developmental experience of the program, and thus somewhat of the economic viability of the program.

ACCREDITATION Notes which agencies and associations accredit the program. SEE: the section on ACCREDITATION further on in this handbook for a detailed description of the importance of, criteria for, and listing of reliable accreditation associations.

Tuition	Listed as complete cost of the program. Effective Rate (ER) noted when possible.
Text Costs	Listed only when not included in overall cost of the program.
Time Limits	Generally vocational programs' time limits are the average time it takes for students to complete the program, and not specific parameters. However, courses/programs offered by colleges and universities most likely adhere to specific time limits. Please refer to the Time Limits criteria in the High School outline for further information in this regard.
Curriculum	A listing of the number of individual or module courses outlining the program, many times with course titles.
Description	A short narrative explaining the purpose, scope, and potential of the program offering.
Comments	This criteria provides program prerequisites and material requirements. Notation of whether incarcerated students are enrolled, and whether college-level credits are granted upon completion.

Paralegal

Program	The title or category of offering from the school.
Certificate	Whether or not a certificate is provided upon completion and what type of certificate, as well as number of CEUs or credit hours awarded upon completion.
Accreditation	Which agencies and associations that accredit the program. See: the section on Accreditation further on in this handbook for a detailed description of the importance of, criteria for, and listing of reliable accreditation associations.
Affiliations	Listing of association memberships which indicate adherence to industry standards.
Tuition	Listed as cost per course or total program fee.

Text Costs   Usually included in overall program cost, if not then as cost per text or for whole program.

Time Limits   Usually provided as average or total program completion time. Proprietary schools usually are less stringent on completion times. If courses are provided by a college or university, however, refer to the Time Limits criteria in the college section outline for more information.

Transfer Hours   Provides you with information if previously earned school credits can be applied to the diploma program, thus reducing the cost and time in fulfilling the number of necessary credits to graduate. And if provided in the program's materials, also includes the number of credits you are allowed to transfer, or conversely the number of credits you must take from the program to graduate. The acceptance of transfer credits is wholly at the discretion of the receiving program, and usually is based on the credits being from an accredited program and the accepting school having a similarly related course. Finally, if the school profiled does not offer a diploma program, there is no need to transfer units to it, and this criteria is simply then noted as: "Non-Applicable."

Curriculum   A listing of the number of individual or module courses outlining the program, many times with course titles.

Description   A short narrative explaining the purpose, scope, and potential of the program offering.

Comments   This criteria provides program prerequisites and material requirements. Notation of whether incarcerated students are enrolled and whether college-level credits are granted upon completion. Special note if graduates are eligible for professional association memberships.

Colleges, Law Schools & Universities

Founded   Date when the school established correspondence study, not necessarily when the school itself was founded. Additional information provided is the academic year from which the profile was derived, e.g. (2007-2008).

Accreditation   Which agencies and associations accredit the school. SEE: the section on Accreditation further on in this handbook for a detailed description of the importance of, criteria for, and listing of reliable accreditation associations.

CERTIFICATION   Listing of certificate/diploma/degree offerings, with number of credit hours required. Areas of Study/Concentration/Majors & Minors listed as well.

TUITION   Listed as per hour of semester-based cost. If school is a quarter-hour-based program, the Effective Rate (ER) calculation provides an across the board program-to-program comparable fee figure for one credit hour/unit. Additional per course or term enrollment and incidental fees are noted.

TEXT COSTS   The most common fluctuating cost between programs due to the books and materials assigned to a particular course. This criteria provides a range from the lowest cost of books for a course to the highest cost for a particular class. More common in the second edition is the average (AVG) cost of texts per course. You will have to write for the program's catalog for specific text costs, but not all school's materials provide this information. You may have to write for a particular course's bibliography and costs. Many schools offer the opportunity to purchase used texts. I have always chosen this option to save money (approximately two-thirds the cost of a new text), and have never been shortchanged on the materials needed for a course.

TIME LIMITS   Lets you know the maximum period you have to complete a course, and where provided, the minimum time in which a course can be completed as well. Remember that these time limits include mailing time, professor evaluation, and return shipping. Common practice is to permit only two lesson submissions at a time though you may be able to negotiate another arrangement. So factor in these time elements in your scheduling. Additional notations indicate if the program offers time extensions and if so the number of, length, and fee for such. Based upon personal experience, the shortest time I ever completed a class from enrollment to final exam (twelve lessons and two proctored exams), was five months and one week. The majority of this time was spent waiting for lesson submissions to be evaluated and returned. I would be hesitant to enroll in a program that does not allow a minimum of nine months for course completion before an extension period needs to be purchased if necessary.

TRANSFER HOURS   Provides you with information if previously earned school credits can be applied to the degree program, thus reducing your cost in fulfilling the number of necessary credits to graduate. And, if provided in the program's materials, also includes the number of credits you are allowed to transfer, or conversely the number of credits you must take from the program to graduate. Additionally, if provided in the materials, this criteria notes the types of equivalency programs, such as ACE, CLEP and DANTES (reviewed further on in this handbook) that are considered for credit acceptance by the school. The acceptance of transfer credits is wholly at the discretion of the receiving program, and usually based on the credits being from an accredited program and the accepting school having a similarly related course. Finally, if the school being outlined does not offer a diploma program, there is no need to transfer units to it, and this criteria is simply then noted as: "Non-Applicable."

COURSES — This lets you know the category and number in each category of the classes offered by the program. For a more detailed description of the individual courses, write to the schools for their catalogs.

COMMENTS — This criteria provides an evaluation of the tuition rates and/or other relevant information that might be of interest to the prisoner-student. Extensive offerings, usually a course category with ten or more classes, is noted for quick reference. Unusual course offerings may also be noted here. If incarcerated students are enrolled this is cited for it advises you that the school has at least some administrative experience in dealing with the unique vagaries in the course of prisoner-student study. Finally, personal comments as to the viability or utility of the program, or reputation of the school, are sometimes provided (for what they are worth).

UNDERGRADUATE TUITION VALUE SCALE*

Up to $100 = Excellent Tuition Rates
$101 to $150 = Very Good Tuition Rates
$151 to $200 = Good Tuition Rates
$106 to $160 = Average Tuition Rates

GRADUATE TUITION VALUE SCALE*

Up to $100 = Excellent Tuition Rates
$101 to $200 = Good Tuition Rates
$201 to $400 = Average Tuition Rates

*Based on Effective Rate of all course and term fees averaged into one semester credit hour. This allows easy comparison of true tuition rates between colleges and universities.

> **"A college education should equip one
> to entertain three things:
> a friend, an idea, and oneself."**
>
> — Thomas Ehrlich

Summation

By utilizing the information provided in the program outlines you can compare and contrast school offerings, narrowing your choices for future research. Once you have identified programs of probable interest, write to the schools requesting their catalogs and materials. Upon receipt you can further reduce your choices to a single program, or if you are compiling a degree program, a few selections.

Factors in Selecting a Program

Prisoner-students selecting a correspondence program are limited by factors that are not of concern to the traditional distance education student.

THE PRISONER-STUDENT is constrained by institutional policies ranging from contraband to property control to educational administration procedures. Before enrolling in any program the prisoner-student should collect and thoroughly review all prison policies relevant to his or her continuing education, and consult with the institution's education director or designee, providing the administrator with all the elected program's materials to review. Have signed approval before enrolling in any program.

The education administrator can be your best ally, smoothing out inevitable glitches, or your worst bureaucratic nightmare by obtusely failing to manage the education program. It is best to thoroughly explain your course of study and follow explicitly whatever instructions and advice the education administrator provides. Keep the administrator updated about your progress. Share well-received term papers and good test scores. You never know what type of assistance you can receive as the administrator comes to believe in your quest as well. Being on the administrator's right side can pay dividends long after your initial enrollment.

Keep copies of all paperwork no matter who it is from. A documented paper trail may well be your only path to salvation if something or someone tries to throw a monkey wrench into your education. Knowing the policies and procedures, maintaining a complete documentation file, and recruiting allies, such as the education administrator, are the best tactics to protect yourself.

Besides making sure the program you select has no requirements (such as a chemistry lab) that will violate your prison's policies and/or be impossible to fulfill (like field trips to an art gallery), you need to determine if you possess the program's or particular course's prerequisites before you attempt to enroll. Prerequisites, such as having a High School Diploma or GED, or taking foundation courses, such as English Composition before being able to take Creative Writing, are listed some-

> "To persevere is always a reflection of the state of one's inner life, one's philosophy and one's perspective."
> — DAVID GUTERSON

where in the school's materials. DO NOT ignore them. If you have questions, or can provide a reason, such as job training or some form of life experience, for the school to waive a particular requirement, submit the request and await resolution before investing your cash.

By making these provisions, the selection of a program is initially based on what you want to accomplish. For example, if you want to earn a Masters of Business Administration (MBA) degree, and do not have a High School Diploma or GED, then that will be your first goal to accomplish. Next you will have to earn an Associate Degree, followed by a Baccalaureate with at least a minor in business studies. The least expensive way to accomplish this would be to earn your GED through your prison's on-site educational program; however, if you have the financial resources and desire, you can earn a High School Diploma via correspondence from a number of fully accredited schools. Then you can select any number of college programs and begin working towards your Associate and Bachelor degrees.

Regardless of the differences in goals, the criteria for program selection remains largely the same. After determining your general goal, the selection of the actual school is based most generally on cost. Once you identify schools that provide your program or courses of choice, cost comparisons can be made by factoring in tuition charges, text costs, and incidental fees. With any acceptable accredited program, costs would be the primary factor when determining my choice between similar courses from different schools.

> "According to the commonest principles of human action, no man will do as much for you as you will do for yourself."
> — Marcus Garvey

Accreditation

Accreditation by a U.S. Department of Education (USDOE) recognized accrediting association assures a student that the accredited school has met certain standards concerning the quality of education, faculty, books and materials, student satisfaction, financial stability, truthful advertising, etc.

THE EVALUATION PROCESS, conducted by an independent agency, is repeated every five years. Not all accredited schools are of the same quality; however, course credits between similarly accredited schools are generally transferable from one school to the other. It is up to the individual educational institution to decide to accept any particular course for transfer credit. In most cases, if a school has the same or similar offering, a transfer from a similarly accredited program will be accepted.

There is not one national all encompassing accrediting agency. Accrediting associations developed regionally as educational institutions were established across the country. Some focus on particular programs, such as religious study. All state sponsored colleges and universities are required by their legislatures to be regionally accredited in order to receive state appropriations. All institutions of higher education receiving any type of federal funding, from research grants to student loans, must also be accredited by a USDOE recognized association. The Distance Education Training Council (DETC)—formerly known as the National Home Study Council—employs procedures similar to those of other USDOC recognized educational accrediting associations, and generally accredits independent and proprietary schools that meet DETC's qualifications.

There are many specific fields of study accrediting agencies, and these focus on particular programs, like architecture, business and nursing, and are taught by departments within a college or university. For the purposes of the prisoner-student, there are eight USDOE recognized accrediting associations that we need to be concerned with. These eight accrediting associations are:

> "All men who have turned out worth anything have had the chief hand in their own education."
>
> — SIR WALTER SCOTT

American Association of Bible Colleges
Distance Education Training Council
Middle States Association of Colleges and Schools
New England Association of Schools and Colleges
North Central Association of Colleges and Schools
Northwest Association of Schools and Colleges
Southern Association of Colleges and Schools
Western Association of Schools and Colleges

> "On the human chessboard, all moves are possible."
> — Miriam Schiff

There are schools that are non-accredited by the previously listed associations. Colleges and universities from Canada and the United Kingdom profiled in this guide are comparably accredited in their countries. There may well be delays, difficulties, or possibly even denials in attempting to transfer academic credit hours to or from these schools to a U.S. program. This is not due to concerns about quality, but rather because of the inherent complications and variances between educational systems in different countries. Ironically, a full degree will be more easily accepted than a comparable number of credits. Still there are some good programs and good tuition fees (factoring in the exchange rate) with the Canadian and UK schools.

Another concern is the rather recent development of the formation of non USDOE recognized accrediting agencies. These companies have been formed to capitalize on the need for proprietary correspondence schools, that cannot meet the standards of the regional accrediting agencies, to "sell" educationally meaningless accreditation. This is why the statement of "accreditation" itself does not guarantee a certain level of quality; such accreditation must be issued by a USDOE recognized association to have any relevant meaning. The World Association of Universities and Colleges, located in Las Vegas, Nevada, is such a private accrediting agency, and is not recognized by the U.S. Department of Education.

It should be noted, however, that not all programs of value are accredited. For various reasons some schools cannot meet all of the accreditation criteria or do not want the restrictions that accreditation can place on a program. Many vocational training programs offer quality instruction and are offered by non-accredited schools. Some colleges and universities are non-accredited, yet federal and state governments, Fortune 500 companies, and multitudes of smaller firms finance their employees' education through these programs. This fact may be a better determinant of workplace viability than program accreditation. It is up to each student to make the determination of what is an acceptable program, and which is not. It is my opinion that if at all possible, the prisoner-student should participate in accredited programs by USDOE recognized accrediting associations.

> "Our life is what our thoughts make it. A man will find that as he alters his thoughts towards things and other people, things and other people will alter towards him."
>
> — JAMES ALLEN

Diploma Mills

A diploma mill is a substandard or fraudulent college or university that offers potential students degrees with little or no serious work.

> "You can't be over-booked, only under-read."
> — John Drybred

SOME ARE SIMPLE FRAUDS with a P.O. Box where you send a check. In return you receive a grandiose diploma and officious looking transcript but that diploma and transcript are worthless. In this instance, both the school and student know that the transaction is a fraudulent one. Other diploma mills require some nominal work from the student but do not require college-level courses normally required for degree fulfillment. These schools may require minimal work, non-proctored exams, offer extensive and easily awarded life-experience credits, and degrees within a short period of time. Naive students can "graduate" from these programs thinking they earned a legitimate degree when it too is actually worthless.

If the answers to many of the following questions are "yes", the degree provider may well be a "diploma mill":

- ✓ Can degrees (diplomas) simply be purchased?
- ✓ Is there a claim of accreditation with no evidence of this status?
- ✓ Is there a claim of accreditation from a non-USDOE recognized agency?
- ✓ Does the school lack state or federal licensure to operate?
- ✓ Are few if any assignments required to earn a degree?
- ✓ Is a very short period of time required to earn a degree?
- ✓ Are there few requirements for students to earn credits?
- ✓ Are degrees available based solely through a P.O. Box or website?
- ✓ Does the school fail to provide a faculty roster and qualifications?
- ✓ Does the school's name sound unfamiliar to other well-known colleges?
- ✓ Does the school make claims for which there is no supporting evidence?

While accreditation by recognized associations confers legitimacy to colleges and universities, not all unaccredited colleges are diploma mills. Some unaccredited colleges provide legitimate academic work. Schools may be undergoing the protracted accreditation process, and others may have chosen not to seek the restrictions of various accrediting regulations. One evaluative tool of unaccredited schools is their use by industry and government agencies for the continuing education of their employees. If Fortune 500 companies and state and federal departments recognize degree completions and/or sponsor their employees through the school's programs, this is a solid indication this particular school is not a diploma mill. A key factor to remember is that in order for a school to be considered a diploma mill it must award degrees with little or no work required.

> "Persistence is the twin sister of excellence. One is the matter of quality; the other, a matter of time."
>
> — MARABEL MORGAN

The Least Expensive Path to a Baccalaureate

The final choice in selecting a program rests with the prisoner-student.

> "I will prepare and someday my chance will come."
> —Abraham Lincoln

WHAT FOLLOWS is a sample outline of how a prisoner-student already possessing a HSD/GED could piece together a baccalaureate program from fully accredited schools, with tuition cost being the primary criteria in selecting the programs.

Louisiana State University
Sam Houston State University

Tuition Rates: $78.00 (AVG) per semester hour: No Correspondence Degree Program (though LSU offers 3 certificate programs that add up to 45 credits that can be applied to Associate and Bachelor Degrees; no reason to pass on them) Categories of Courses: Accounting, Agriculture, Anthropology, Biological Sciences, Business Law, Chemistry, Communication Studies, Economics, English, Environmental Studies, Family & Consumer Sciences, Finance, French, Geography, Geology, German, Health, History, Human Resource Education, Kinesiology, Latin, Psychology, Sociology, Spanish, Statistics.

90 semester credit hours: = $7020.00 Texts (AVG: $60.00) & Incidental fees (approximated) = $1980.00

The basic concept is to take as many courses as possible from the lowest tuition schools, eventually transferring the maximum-allowable credit hours to the cheapest degree granting programs. With this in mind, the following outline is the least expensive correspondence course method to earn a baccalaureate from fully-accredited schools. This outline is actually divided into two separate programs. One focuses on a liberal arts curriculum, the other is theologically based.

JON MARC TAYLOR

Adams State College

Bachelor of Arts/Science (120 hours)

Tuition Rate (ER: 120.00) BA/S in Business/Interdisciplinary Studies/Sociology

120 semester credit hours: = $14,400.00 Texts (AVG: $60.00) & Incidental fees (approximated) = $900.00

TOTAL ESTIMATED COST OF BACCALAUREATE (2007-2008 fee schedules): $15,360

Global University

Bachelor of Arts (128 hours)

Tuition Rate: (ER: $82.53) Factoring in 20% Prisoner Discount!

Areas of Concentration: Bible, Theology, Religious Education, Missions, Bible/Pastoral Ministries & Honors degrees

128 semester credit hours: = $10,563.84 Texts (AVG: $84.00) & Incidental fees (approximated): = $3936.16

TOTAL ESTIMATED COST OF BACCALAUREATE (2000-2001 fee schedule): $14,500.00

Both of these program outlines are from the curriculum of accredited USDOE recognized schools. The latter outline from Global University has a Christian theological curriculum, and for those seeking greater religious-oriented insight and knowledge, or perhaps a career calling in ministry/pastoral work, this program is a "Best Buy" for the prisoner-student. Besides the special prisoner-discount that Global offers, the school also provides free continuing education courses to prisoners. All anecdotal information I have about this school has been of a positive nature.

The first program curriculum is liberal arts based. This is your traditional collegiate course of study. From a Canadian school's catalog, I have never come across a better description of what this epistemology entails and strives to achieve:

The liberal arts education

A liberal arts education will give you a greater awareness and understanding of human development and endeavor, of human social, political, economic, cultural activity, of history, values, beliefs and knowledge

> "Measure your mind's height by the shade it casts."
>
> — ELIZABETH BARRETT BROWNING

systems, of societies, literatures and languages, and of the physical world in which we live.

Moreover, you will have the opportunity to develop and refine your intellectual skills in achieving this education. You will extend your ability to understand new information and hypothesize, to find and interpret information relevant to an issue or question, to analyze problems critically and objectively, and to communicate effectively.

A liberal arts education is highly individual. Your program and course selection should reflect your own interests and abilities.

Cost increases

As a final note, for those who reference the first edition of this guide, you will note a near doubling of the cost between that edition's least expensive path to a baccalaureate and the second edition's. When referencing the second edition of PGH to this edition, you will note a 35% to 45% increase in this process. Between the first and third editions of this handbook, the cost of a bachelor's degree has thus doubled. These are perfect examples of the continuously increasing cost of distance education opportunities.

Time to get busy!

Between the second edition and this update, Taylor University, with its then-generous prisoner-student tuition discount offer (i.e., ER: $69.00), has eliminated its correspondence program altogether. Thus, between the first edition, with which you could have earned an Associate Degree from Taylor University with an ER of $25 per credit, the degree program was eliminated (due to a web-based course requirement.) Then the study option via correspondence was eliminated altogether. Another changing factor between the previous edition and this version in overall program cost increase is that of Texas Tech University's 60% tuition rate increase, making it more expensive than the least expensive baccalaureate degree program from the second edition. This is a continuing example that it is time to get busy! Each semester you delay, the more expensive your end degree becomes. Fees will continue to increase and the cost of your BA is only getting more expensive.

> "We can change our circumstances by a mere change of our attitude."
> — WILLIAM JAMES

There is a third lower-cost option, at least for earning an Associate Degree. Ashworth University, a DETC accredited institution, offers the best ER tuition rate of $20.00 a credit hour and this includes texts! It seems almost too good to be true, but I have corresponded with an ex-federal parolee who graduated from Ashworth during her bit. She was pleased with the courses, felt they were adequate college-level work, and reports that the credits are accepted for transfer by some schools and not others. The school also has monthly payment plans, and if you reside in a prison system that permits entering into such contracts (like the Bureau of Prisons), this could be your "Best-Buy" for an Associate Degree. My concern though arises if and when you attempt matriculation to a BA degree program, will that school recognize and accept these credits? This is a factor you need to take into consideration.

> "Our real wealth is in the intangible power of thought."
> — NAPOLEON HILL

Other College-Level Credit Sources

Other recognized college-level credit sources can save you literally thousands of dollars.

> "There is never a better measure of what a person is than what he becomes when he's absolutely free to choose."
> — WILLIAM M. BULGER

THESE OTHER SOURCES occur through on-the-job training (e.g., NIASE-Automotive Service Excellence Examinations are worth 19-42 credits), military experience (e.g., Boot Camp is worth between 1-3 physical education credits) and schools (e.g., MP School is worth 3 criminal justice credits), independent self-education, and general life experience to mention just a few of the possibilities. These areas can be valuable experiences and translate into recognized college credits, which save you money by reducing the number of courses you need to take.

There are various ways to achieve this transformation. Noted in the schools' profiles throughout this guide, in the TRANSFER HOURS criteria, these various methods acceptable to particular schools are noted as ACE, ACT-PEP, CLEP, DANTES, Experiential or Learning Portfolio, Life Experience, etc. Even if a school does not have such a notation, or a particular method is not listed, it does not mean the school would not be amenable to such a crediting process. You have nothing to lose, and possibly many thousands of dollars to save, in writing for more information in this regard. Schools can be very accommodating in creating a degree program; it just depends on their philosophy and counseling staff. What follows are brief descriptions of these various non-traditional credit accumulation means.

ACE/CREDIT or ACE/PONSI are specific numbers of semester-based credit hours recommended by the American Council on Education/College Credit Recommendation Service, which evaluates and makes credit recommendations for formal educational programs and courses sponsored by non-collegiate organizations that are non-degree granting and that offer courses to their employees, members or customers. Courses with ACE/CREDIT recommendation require supervised (i.e., proctored) examinations, and require a minimum (i.e., 70%) higher combined grade for all assignments and examinations. These credit recommendations are intended to guide colleges and universities as they consider awarding credit to persons who have successfully completed non-collegiate sponsored instruction (e.g., GRADUATE SCHOOL USDA offers many ACE-credit courses at a good price). Over 1000 colleges and universities throughout the United States have accepted ACE-credit recommendations as part of their regular non-traditional credit evaluation processes (Refer to Index for a sample listing). For more information regarding this service contact:

> Registry of Credit Recommendation
> American Council on Education
> One Dupont Circle, N.W., Suite 250
> Washington, D.C. 20036-1193

CLEP is the College-Level Examinations Program administered by the College Entrance Examination Board. CLEP provides a reliable and effective means for colleges and universities to grant credit, placement, and exemption by examination to their students. There are five general and twenty-nine subject CLEP exams that currently represent courses typical of the first two years of college study, stressing the areas of liberal arts and business. More than 2,800 accredited institutions of higher education award credit for satisfactory scores on CLEP examinations. This is the good news. Now here is the bad.

CLEP exams, along with DANTES exams, are structurally irrelevant to prisoner-students. In 2003/2004 the College Entrance Examination Board eliminated the traditional pencil and paper exam method, and instead became a solely online testing service. This change also resulted in the elimination of the "special needs" student (which included prisoners) testing fee waiver program, which had make CLEP/DANTES exams cost-free to prisoners. The fee waiver program had provided prisoner-students with the opportunity to accumulate numerous credits at very little cost, limited only by their study habits.

> College-Level Examination Program
> Post Office Box 6600
> Princeton, NJ 08541-6600

DANTES, now called DSST (DANTES Subject Standardized Tests), the Defense Activity for Non-Traditional Education Support program is sim-

> "The voyage of discovery is not in seeking new landscapes, but in having new eyes."
> —MARCEL PROUST

ilar to CLEP examinations. While previously only available to active duty military or current reserve and guard personnel, the tests are now available to anyone. More than 1,200 colleges and universities award credit for DANTES completions. There are thirty-seven subject tests in six areas of study, costing about the same as CLEP exams. Again, the same testing problem exists in the requirement of Special Testing Centers establishment before a prisoner-student can take these exams; however, many ex-service personnel have acquired these designations and can utilize them in prior learning credit accumulation. For this reason, and probably ACE-credit recommendations for the Military Occupation Specialty (MOS) qualifications, every former service member should submit a notarized copy of their DD214s for training credit recognition. I did so, reducing by a few credits the courses I needed to earn my bachelors degree.

Dantes Program
P.O. Box 6604
Princeton, NJ 08541

ACT-PEP, now known as Regents Examinations, are similar to CLEP and DANTES exams. These forty-two subject tests are accepted by nearly 1,000 colleges and universities. While nearly three times more expensive than CLEP or DANTES examinations, they do cover subjects at the junior and senior levels, which the other equivalency programs do not, as well as subjects not covered by CLEP or DANTES tests. Thus, Regents Exams are particularly attractive to students needing a few upper-level credits to fulfill a degree program. The unknown factor as of this writing is the testing procedure utilized. If Regents (Excelsior) College has adopted online testing as its sole delivery medium, then the same structural problem exists. If anyone has employed this method, regardless of the outcome, I would very much like to learn of your experience. For more information contact:

Regents College Examinations
7 Columbia Circle
Albany, NY 12203

Learning/Experiential Portfolio Assessment can also encompass the terms of Life Experience credits and other synonyms. Portfolio Assessment provides the most flexible option for earning college credits. Through this process, your knowledge and skills can very often be translated into college credits. Areas in which you may have earned college-level knowledge include, but are not limited to: employment experience and training, volunteer work, adult education courses, seminars, workshops, military service, travel, community service, hobbies, personal reading, published writings, and a plethora of other life experiences. Life Experience credits may be awarded for activities that have serious or artistic merit, are conducted consistently for at least 135 hours per year, require intensive personal commitment, are directly supervised by individuals who possess a high level of professional expertise in the relevant subject area, and are marked by attainment of an appreciable degree of accomplishment.

The portfolio allows you to demonstrate to an expert in the field what knowledge you possess in a particular course area. It is often compiled like a notebook or chapbook, with each portfolio generally representing one course. Components of a portfolio include: request for experiential learning credit (possibly utilizing the school's form), table of contents, autobiography, resume, degree plan, significant learning outline, narrative, bibliography and supporting documentation. What is integral in the portfolio is the completeness and accuracy documenting your life experience, leadership and responsibility of positions held, awards received, continuing educational conferences attended, and resulting change to life effectiveness and use of resources available. Since, though, there is no set design for this assessment, each school utilizing the method will provide instructions as to its actual composition.

Finally, this process is not cost free. Schools may charge anywhere from a one-time overall fee to a set rate per credit hour granted. This fee, however, is usually substantially less than standard tuition rates. Adams State College (exampled earlier in this chapter) offers an "unofficial" evaluation for free, which attempts to show you where your previous credits fit into the school's degree requirements. This unofficial evaluation, however, does not guarantee these credits will be accepted for transfer. In addition, life experience credits accepted by a school are non-transferable to other colleges or universities; you will have to reapply through the same process at each school.

For more information on this option contact:

Council for Adult & Experiential Learning
55 East Monroe Street, Suite 1930
Chicago, IL 60613

"Portfolio Video Seminar & Printed Study Guide"
Follet's Bookstore
Governors State University (IL)
1-800-GSU-8GSU, ext. 4588

Experiential Learning Guidebook
William Kemble
National College Studies
675 Blue Mountain Road
Saugerties, NY 12477

End of Course Exams, also called "Course Credit-by-Examination" among other labels, is an educational structure similar to CLEP and DANTES exams, except in this case, the credits granted are usually for a more specific course in a college curriculum. This method is of particular use when one or a few designated courses are necessary to fill out a degree program's requirement.

These exams are basically the same tests that are used in the traditional correspondence program. The value in utilizing this option is in reduced expenses and less time invested. In the typical situation, the expense of Credit-by-Examination courses is from one-third to one-half what traditional per-credit-hour enrollment costs at the issuing school.

In most programs you can enroll in these courses (which at some schools are the same ones available for traditional correspondence study), purchase the study guide, syllabus and texts, schedule your end-of-course exams when you are ready. There are no assignments or mid-terms to complete; you study in preparation to pass the single end-of-course exam. For most students, the selection of a particular class using these means is based upon a particular need for the transcript credit, usually to fulfill a minor or major area of study.

Additional costs can be saved by either purchasing deeply discounted used and/or older editions of the course's texts, maybe being lucky enough to find the text or similar book in your prison library, or sharing books with other students at your prison taking the same exams. You can establish a study group, with each student delegated to acquiring texts for various courses, and then sharing your resources and experiences. Leverage by every means your resources to advance your education.

Two schools that offer extensive Credit-by-Examination courses:

Ohio University
Office of Independent Study
Tupper Hall
Athens, OH 45701-2979
(168 course options)

University of North Carolina
Independent Studies
CB-1020 The Friday Center
Chapel Hill, NC 27599-1020
(108 course options)

CEU (Continuing Education Units) is a nationally recognized standard unit of measurement, established by the Council on Continuing Education Unit, that provides a permanent record of your lifelong learning experiences. One CEU is defined as "10 contact hours of participation in an organized continuing education experience under responsible sponsorship, with capable direction and qualified instructors." A standard formula for converting semester and quarter college and university credits to CEUs is as follows:

Semester Credits:
1 Undergraduate Credit Hour = 4.8 CEUs
1 Graduate Credit Hour = 6.4 CEUs
Quarter Credit:
1 Undergraduate Credit Hour = 3.2 CEUs
1 Graduate Credit Hour = 5.0 CEUs

While college credits can be readily computed into acceptable CEUs, the reverse is not necessarily the case. A CEU granting course or program may be used in Life Experience or Portfolio Assessment, but such a credit evaluation is thoroughly within the discretion of the accepting school.

> "At twenty-two, I thought I knew everything. Now at sixty-seven, I find I haven't tasted a drop from the sea of knowledge. The more I learn, the more I find out how little I know."
>
> — JOHN E. COPAGE

Managing Your Education

Course Management: Once you have selected your program of study, identified a school or schools to enroll, and obtained all the necessary authorizations, comes the task of actually taking the course.

SOME TIPS on taking a class may help you avoid some of the problems others, including myself, have encountered in correspondence study. To begin with, when your materials arrive, take inventory of the package to make sure everything is included: curriculum guide/workbook, texts, mailing labels, etc. If not, follow-up with a letter to the school noting the missing items. If the missing materials prevent you from beginning study, the course's time limits should not commence until all necessary items are available. (Keep good records as they might be necessary.)

Second, thoroughly review all the program's instructions. Learn everything from time limits, to number of lessons that can be submitted at one time, how lessons are to be shipped, and any special instructions, such as requiring lessons to be typed (this may be waived if you write explaining your circumstances), in lesson preparation. Third, set yourself a schedule for completing each lesson or set of lessons. Allow yourself some buffer time to compensate for all unexpected delays that inevitably seem to pop up in the penitentiary.

> "Adversity causes some men to break, others to break records."
> — WILLIAM ARTHUR WARD

Time Management will be one of your most important study skills.

Fourth, if at all possible, type your lessons and keep a carbon (cheaper in most cases than photocopying) of the assignments in your course files. Fifth, make sure your return address on the mailing envelope is CLEARLY printed, and the mailing address is in accordance with the instructions from the school. If a lesson is not returned in thirty days, send a query letter to see if it arrived at all. Sixth, keep all graded lessons and tests in your course file. You can use these for test preparation, thesis research, and as examples, i.e. proof, of your efforts to anyone who might matter to you—like dear old Mum. I have shipped all of my texts, lessons, and papers home over the years. Build yourself a personal library with your program materials.

Finally, just use common sense when managing your courses, always trouble shooting the worst possible scenarios, and how you would rectify them. Always have a back up plan. Think through these situations and you should be able to successfully manage your correspondence courses.

CURRICULUM CONSTRUCTION: In vocational and paralegal study programs your curriculum is usually quite clearly set forth for you by the school. They tell you what courses you must take to fulfill the program's requirements. In high school and college programs, however, curriculum construction is less direct and more implicit. The student has the ultimate responsibility in completing all the requirements to graduate. Each diploma or degree program, somewhere in the materials you receive, will set forth what particular courses — usually known as core courses—must be taken, and the areas and number of credits/units that must be completed as well. Schools provide curriculum counselors, but the quality of service and personal attention can vary widely. In the end, it is your responsibility to meet graduation requirements. It is especially important for the student to know curriculum requirements when piecing together a degree from a multitude of sources. The following is a sample curriculum outline from Texas Tech University's Bachelor of General Studies Degree:

GENERAL REQUIREMENTS: (58 hours)
English, Introductory Courses (6 hours)
Oral Communication (3 hours)
Political Science (6 hours)
History (6 hours)
Mathematics/Logical Reasoning (6 hours)
Natural Science (8 hours)
Technology/Applied Science (3 hours)
Social/Behavioral Sciences (3 hours)
Humanities/Fine Arts (6 hours)
Foreign Language (0-10 hours)
Multicultural Requirement (chosen from approved list)
AREAS OF CONCENTRATION: (54 hours)

"Always bear in mind that your own resolution to succeed is more important than any other thing."

— ABRAHAM LINCOLN

Choose three areas from:

Business/Communication/English/History or Mathematics/Minimum of 18 hours each area, including 6 hours at 300/400 level

Elective courses will be whatever other courses might be needed:

(a) to have a total of at least 125 hours,

(b) at least 90 hours from Arts & Sciences, and

(c) at least 45 hours of advanced 300/400 level courses. Also, the 125 total must include 6 hours from any two courses designated as "Writing Intensive."

Each diploma or degree program has its own requirements, but are similarly constructed. Be sure you understand these requirements and have a plan on how to fulfill them. If your school does not provide you with a personal curriculum sheet, then construct your own, filling in each completed course in the appropriate areas. For each semester's worth of credits, request an updated curriculum sheet from your diploma/degree program to verify your own records.

FINANCING: Finding funds is the biggest challenge for the prisoner-student. With the expulsion of prisoners from the Pell Grant program, half the on-site prison college programs ceased to exist. The remainder have withered, even more subsequently ceasing operations, and all seeking other funding sources. There are some remarkable reemerging opportunities, such as Bard Prison Initiative in New York and the Prison University Project in San Quentin. Hurrah for them! In those systems that closed their classroom doors, however, the only option for higher education is via correspondence study. At this time, I know of no source of scholarship or grant funding for prisoners to continue their education in prison systems that do not already offer PSCE opportunities. That is save one promising program, which I will report on later in this section.

All is not lost. There are ways to raise funds and there are a few schools offering scholarships. The first option is naturally your own resources of savings or income from prison jobs (for those that have them that pay more than pennies on the hour). For most of us, though, all savings were exhausted in the legal process, and state tips do not even come close in covering the necessities of daily life. The next possible source is friends and family members. Even if you do not accept deposits into your trust account from them, or they do not wish to donate to your prison lifestyle, when it comes to furthering your education theirs and your attitude can change. If prison policies allow, have them pay the tuition and

> "Once you are really challenged, you find something in yourself. Man doesn't know what he is capable of until he is asked."
>
> — KOFI ANNAN

text costs directly to the schools. As long as educational materials arrive prepaid at most prisons, directly from the vendor, this is allowed. But double check your institution's policies on this point.

Other sources of possible funding are church and service groups. I financed my graduate degree by writing to churches throughout the state seeking tuition assistance. Explaining who I was, where I was, and what I was trying to accomplish, many congregations graciously supported my quest. Included in my mailing were copies of my transcripts, resume, and references. Finally, I arranged for my mentor to receive and disburse all educational funds. This moderated suspicions of a scam, and recruited an outside advocate for the cause of my education. There are literally thousands of congregations and hundreds of service groups in each state. Arrange a contact package that best presents your cause, is designed to alleviate as many fears from the recipients' minds as possible, and is as simple a plan that will work in the circumstances you are constrained within.

In Indiana, I had a success rate of two-percent of contacted churches sponsoring at least one or more classes. In Missouri, on the other hand, utilizing the refined contact package, I could not enlist a single sponsor out of three-hundred-plus churches contacted. This is a feasible option, but one that will require the investment of more of your time and attention raising funds than you will probably spend studying. Just a hard fact in our hard lives.

Regarding this solicitation strategy, Ohio University's College Program for the Incarcerated (CPI) prints the following in their prisoner-specific catalog:

"The only other avenue for those who need financial aid is to seek it from a charitable group, institution, or business. Many civic, church, service, and professional groups have been successfully approached by our students. Often when a group understands the benefit of earning college credit for an incarcerated student, it will be willing to offer some financial assistance, even if on a limited basis. CPI does not intend to suggest that locating such aid is easy and does not have a list of groups, but the number of students who have met success in obtaining aid is encouraging. CPI can accept third-party payments."

One caution: Please be sure such solicitation of aid is permitted by the student's correctional institution.

There are also a few schools that offer distance education scholarships. The one that I know the most about is offered by the University of Colorado at Boulder's Division of Continuing Education and Professional Studies. Each scholarship assists in paying a percentage (30%) of the tuition charges for one course to a maximum of $600.00. There are a limited number of such scholarships awarded each term, and they are issued on first-come first-served basis. They are also limited to one per student, but a guy I am getting ready to introduce you to has received three of these scholarships. He accomplished this by creative presentations, persistence, and a will of not taking "no" for the final answer. Read the COMMENTS section of each outline for programs that offer scholarships. Contact the programs for their procedures. Follow them. Adhere to the deadlines. And never give up.

Dirk Van Velzen is a unique guy. Reminds me of myself fifteen years ago. Serving a ten-year bit out of Washington, Dirk enrolled in Penn State's World Campus before it went totally online. Like all of us he scrambled for funding, and was shocked and then dismayed that prisoners were excluded from Pell Grants, barred from student loans, and left adrift by most correctional education systems. In 2004 he started the Prison Scholarship Fund to raise money for his own education. When family came forward to support his educational pursuits, Dirk redirected the funds to help other prisoner-students. Sitting in prison, Dirk's funding source provided over $1,000 in scholarships for 2006, and $5,000 in prisoner-student financing in 2007.

While funding your education will most likely be your most difficult task in continuing your education, it is not impossible. Be creative. Be persistent. And be honest in where you are, what you want to accomplish, and how you progress. You will be surprised by the amount of support you can receive when you believe in yourself and strive valiantly towards your dreams. Share your grades and papers with your friends, family and sponsors. Seek to include them with your life and success. I have been blessed to make many lifelong friends in my search for funding. I hope you are as lucky. Never give up looking for ways to achieve your dream.

ACADEMIC EXCELLENCE: There are many ways in which we are measured, or "evaluated" in prison. Few of them, however, make note of positive accomplishments. Something that surprised me when I first began my educational odyssey was how important grades became in judging my own self-worth. With time to focus and voracious dedication to learn, you can earn grades that will astound you. Each semester or term, most colleges and universities recognize students taking a minimum number of hours (usually nine or more), and achieving a grade point average to a certain standard (usually 3.6 or better on a 4.0 scale) with "Dean's List" distinction. Make this a goal.

For those students persevering to complete a baccalaureate degree, and earning a certain overall high grade point average, degrees are awarded with academic distinctions so noted on the diploma. These academic honors range, in order of ascending distinction, from Cum Laude to Magna Cum Laude to Summa Cum Laude. These are real distinctions, something of which to be truly proud.

Finally, while each field of study has its honor society, recognizing the very top ranked students in the disciplines, one exists for outstanding distance education students. The Distance Education and Training Council Board of Trustees officially established the Delta Epsilon Tau (DET) Honor Society. DET membership brings honor and earned recognition to individuals who have worked diligently to acquire new knowledge and skills from an accredited distance learning institution. The fact that an individual is elected to membership sets him or her apart from other students and clearly demonstrates a serious commitment to distance education and self-study. For more information contact:

Distance Education & Training Council
Delta Epsilon Tau
1601 18th Street, NW
Washington, DC 20009

CHECKLIST: Blackstone Career Institute offers an excellent paralegal training program and has extensive experience in working with prisoner-students across the nation. Amongst their materials they provide a "Student/Inmate Guide to Enrollment: Getting Started" brochure. Amid the practical information offered is that "It is important to understand that it remains the responsibility of the prospective student to be aware of your facility's own rules, regulations, and policies regarding enrollment." The brochure also outlines the following good checklist:

- ✓ My facility allows participation in correspondence programs.
- ✓ I have received approval from the appropriate staff.
- ✓ I have arranged for tuition payments, either through my own account or someone else's.
- ✓ I have researched whether or not the facility allows for payment plans.
- ✓ If I do need to pay in full, I have asked whether all books can be shipped at once.
- ✓ I have found out whether there are limitations on the number of books/materials I can receive at one time.
- ✓ I have asked whether the shipment of educational materials into my facility requires additional approval or documentation.
- ✓ I know whether the educational materials can be shipped to me or require a third party recipient at my institution.
- ✓ The address on my enrollment application provides adequate information and any special instructions to get my shipments to my location.

How Independent Learning Works:

1. Choose a course(s).
2. Fill out the enrollment application.
3. Order your course materials.
4. Review the course materials in your enrollment package.
5. Work at your own pace, but be aware of time limits.
6. Complete and submit the first assignment.
7. Complete and submit all assignments, generally no more than two at a time.

8. Complete and submit examination requests in proper sequence.
9. Complete your examination.
10. Record your course grade.
11. Review your experiences and learn from them.

> "To be conscious that you are ignorant of the facts is a great step to knowledge."
> — BENJAMIN DISRAELI

Words to the Wise:

A large and growing body of research attests to the fact that you are most likely to succeed at independent study if you begin your work right away.

Success in distance education requires greater self-discipline than the typical classroom course.

It is recommended that you break the course down and set goals for yourself (e.g., complete a lesson and read the next assignment per week, etc.).

Remember you are in charge and responsible for your own progress.

If you need help, contact your institution education staff and/or program counselor.

Study Tips

Beginning something new like correspondence study may cause you some anxiety, particularly if you have not had much success with past educational endeavors. Don't worry. A bit of nervous energy is normal. Combining your nervous energy, motivation, and positive attitude with the study skills outlined here may enhance your learning experience. While you take your correspondence course remember to:

- ✓ Set realistic goals. Plan an initial routine and establish how long it will take you to complete each lesson, based upon the experience in doing so with the first lesson.

- ✓ Encourage and reward yourself along the way. Reward yourself with something special after completing specific goals, such as completion of lessons, assignments or exams. Visualize yourself successfully completing your course.

- ✓ Establish an environment where and when you can study as uninterrupted as possible. Perhaps the prison library. Perhaps late at night. Perhaps when the unit is out to work or recreation, or while wearing headphones to drown out the chaotic noise.
- ✓ Prepare a realistic study plan. Before beginning, take a minute or two to relax and then look at the plan you've developed and visualize yourself completing it successfully. Review previous material, preview new material, and attach significance to what you are learning.
- ✓ Don't be afraid to contact your instructor in addition to what the assignments require. If you have questions, complaints or suggestions, most instructors appreciate the additional communication, because most students fail to interact at all beyond the assignments.
- ✓ Submit clearly written work, preferably typed. When you reveal your rationale for arriving at certain conclusions, your instructor will have a better understanding of what you did and why.

Most importantly, remember you are not alone. The school's continuing education staff and instructors are there to help you. Utilize them!

Anti-Procrastination Tips:

- ✓ Get organized – make a list of what needs to get done.
- ✓ Prioritize your list, and determine how long it will take to accomplish each task.
- ✓ Divide each major task into achievable chunks.
- ✓ Get a calendar and assign time in your schedule to complete each chunk.
- ✓ Schedule reward time – it'll keep your mind on task, instead of thinking, "I wish I was..."

The Highly Productive Learner:

Author Steven Covey's book about the seven habits of highly productive people has helped many people get more accomplished in the work-

> "Goals are dreams with deadlines."
> — DIANA SCHARF

place. Your education IS your job, and Covey's ideas are adaptable to the needs of the adult learner.

1. Be Proactive: It's better to prevent a problem that you see coming than to react to one that has already occurred; this is being pro-active. What could keep you from accomplishing today's study goal? What can you do to make sure this sabotage stops before it begins?

2. Begin with the End in Mind: The end or long term goal is your degree. Keep this in mind as you plan your learning time on a daily, weekly and monthly basis. With each major step, such as a course or major paper completion, take time to congratulate yourself. Visualize yourself looking at your diploma or getting the promotion that the new degree puts within your grasp.

3. Put First Things First: To prioritize sounds easier than it is. Most of us tend to work on easier things first instead of on the things that most need to be completed. As you plan your daily learning time, ask yourself what needs to be done first/today. Think of the tough stuff as the main course and the easy things as dessert.

4. Think Win/Win: Develop and maintain and attitude that seeks to benefit both parties, yourself and others involved.

5. Seek First to Understand, Then to be Understood: Be the best student you can be. Seek knowledge and learn all you can when you study. Don't seek to do as little as possible but rather, as much as necessary. The longer, more encompassingly informed your essay answers (the standard kind in correspondence courses) are in general, the better your grades will be. The more you know on a subject, the better it is for your grades, and your life. Remember: Knowledge Is Power.

6. Synergize: Keep an open mind and listen to what your professors are telling you. The best learning outcomes are the result of teamwork created by the student (your fellow classmates if you are lucky enough to have some) and the teacher.

7. Renewal: Covey says that the four dimensions of human nature are physical, mental, spiritual and social/emotional. If we pay attention to the needs of these dimensions, our capacity to work will be maximized.

Create Your Own University

I want to introduce you to the third prisoner who has done inspirational work in correctional education. His name is William B. Hall. Already possessing an undergraduate degree and a plethora of artistic and business experience, he well knew the value of education. Taking the 2nd edition of PGH, Bill crafted a seminar on "Post-Secondary Education while Incarcerated" at FCC Petersburg. It took six months to convince the administrators to approve the project, but after the first seminar, Bill writes "it went over big time! Now they are setting up additional seminars for me to give." Moreover, at least three of the attendees initiated their own distance education programs. Mr. Hall may quite well be onto something here.

Using PGH, Bill crafted a handout (sometimes directly copying pages from the book) and adding other informative inserts. His objective was to "give inmates a comprehensive review of the various forms of post-secondary education, college and university classes available." The two hour seminar outline is as follows:

Introduction to Post-Secondary Education

- ✓ Degrees offered
- ✓ Accreditation
- ✓ Enrollment requirements

Distance Learning Correspondence Classes

- ✓ Degree seeking
- ✓ Non-degree seeking
- ✓ Certificates

> "Most people search high and wide for the keys to success. If they only knew, the key to their dreams lies within."
> — George Washington Carver

- ✓ Transfer credits
- ✓ Testing for credits
- ✓ Credit for life experience/portfolio construction development

Financing Your Education

- ✓ Tuition and variations in per-hour cost
- ✓ Free-world students vs. incarcerated students
- ✓ Transitions in Pell Grants & other forms of aid
- ✓ Family and community support
- ✓ Books and miscellaneous fees

Getting started

- ✓ Understanding curriculum/core study and major
- ✓ Schools offering academic advisors
- ✓ Time scheduling (pacing yourself without overdoing it)
- ✓ Coordinate with continuing education upon release
- ✓ Interlibrary loan and research
- ✓ Enjoy your studying and keep your "eyes on the prize..."

Jorea Blount is a federal ex-prisoner. While at FCI-Danbury, she was able to institute an ACE (American Council on Education accredited courses) training program in Non-Profit Management and Grantsmanship, utilizing quality training materials provided by the National Social Rehabilitation & Re-Entry Program (Refer to the SJM Family Foundation in the Vocational Section). Jorea writes that "the program is good for someone who doesn't know about nonprofits or grants and doesn't have access to the Internet. It offers the inmate-participant an opportunity to learn something new so upon release they can do a number of things, such as (a) volunteer and give back to the community, (b) expand on what they learned by taking an entry-level job at a nonprofit, and (c) continue their education through formal enrollments."

 Ms. Blount goes on to explain the process in the federal system (which can be used as a model by those of us in state systems) on how to present a course approval application to the administration. In the BOP one fills out a specific application, submits a resume explaining the qualifications to instruct in the class, and provides course outlines, copies of previous education (i.e., transcripts, etc.) and actual course material for review. In this particular instance, the class was held twice a week for two hours.

And as many of us know, so much depends upon the personal vagaries of the administrative personnel we must seek authorization from and interact with for any idea to become successfully enacted. Jorea mentioned that she would not have been able to teach the courses "without the assistance and approval of the Education Coordinator at Federal Correctional Institution-Danbury."

This leads me to this suggestion. To all of you residing in institutions with approachable to open-minded administrators, why not propose the creation of your own university.

Utilizing the CLEP/DANTES Special Testing Center program, have your institution apply for that status. Conduct a "community needs" survey, finding out who is interested in college-level education, and who possesses degrees and in what fields. Hold a seminar coalescing student needs into a few areas of study (e.g., history, psychology, paralegal studies), further identifying potential instructors in those courses. Obtain the CLEP/DANTES study guides for the courses. Purchase past editions of the recommended text books via major distributors. These can be picked up for a few dollars a volume. Use these as loaners to the students and thus they will be available at no additional expense to students the next time the course is taught. Establish a semester schedule, and allow the prisoner-instructors to develop lesson plans and deliver classroom instruction, just like at a regular campus. For students, especially those with little to no higher education experience, the discipline of regularly scheduled classroom sessions, with instructors to guide, answer questions, note progress and give evaluation quizzes, and the interaction of their fellow classmates, will all be critical for their equivalency exam test preparation. At the end of your term, administer the appropriate CLEP/DANTES exams. Those that meet the scoring threshold will have earned a number of recognized and transferable college credits.

Of course this idea will not work at many institutions because of the attitude and quality of the staff. But there are facilities with insightful and even courageous administrators who will be receptive to this concept.

Essential resources

The essential resources are administrative cooperation and support, time and meeting space, and basic financing. Administrators will have to authorize the program. Volunteer clerks can largely organize the internal logistics under administrative supervision. Classroom space for seminar, instruction and testing will have to be allocated and scheduled. Funds for the purchase of course texts and particularly testing fees will have to be raised. And if the CLEP/DANTES testing program structure won't work, investigate the same concept using End-of-Course Exams from Ohio and/or North Carolina Universities.

There is free material from 5,000 courses at more than 150 colleges and universities from around the world. These free open courseware materials include outlines, quizzes and videotaped lectures. Imagine providing instruction for Physics 101 based on the MIT course outline and selected lectures! Access to these, and I cannot emphasize enough, FREE services can be found at:

www.oercommons.org
uocwa.org

Funding is always the crux of the issue with correctional education. Each system is different, and each institution within the system is unique. Perhaps funds can be allocated from the inmate recreation/welfare fund supported by commissary profits and telephone rebates. Maybe the library could purchase 30 retired editions of each of the selected courses. This could be accomplished for less than $200, including shipping charges. The librarian, experienced in the book distribution industry, should be knowledgeable in achieving this outcome. Perhaps inmate service groups, such as the Jaycees, Toastmasters, NAACP, and VVA, could donate sums to the project. Or you could form your own student organization and operate your own fundraisers. Perhaps you could require each student to invest a sum (e.g., $10/20 for each exam taken) to partially cover the cost. This would be a substantial investment for many prisoners living off state wages, and largely eliminate those not wholly involved in earning their education. Any combination of these, or completely different ideas, could work to support your very own, homegrown college program.

Here is a synergistic idea. As a pilot program establishing that such a prisoner-centered teaching program can succeed, institute the Nonprofit Management and Grantsmanship training program as previously mentioned. Employ the skills learned to not only better organize your university, but to seek funding using the techniques learned. By doing so you will have successfully executed a demonstration project of your overarching concept and also exposed your cadre of motivated instructors and students to the skills for achieving your collective dream.

If I was at an institution with a supportive administrator and motivated prisoners I would attempt this project. It's your education. Dream. Dream big. And so what if you fail. At least you tried and you will be stronger for it. The next time around you will succeed.

High School Outlines

American School
2200 East 170th Street, Lansing MI 60438
708-418-2800

CATALOG INFO	2007 (since 1897)
ACCREDITATION	North Central Association of Colleges & Schools / Commission on International & Trans Regional Accreditation
DIPLOMA	General High School Diploma (16 Carnegie Units) College Preparatory Diploma (16 Carnegie Units)
COLLEGE CO-CREDITS	No
TUITION	$100.00 – $220.00 per individual course / $589.00 12th Grade (ER: $73.62) $789.00 11th & 12th Grades $989.00 10th, 11th, & 12th Grades $1,189.00 9th, 10th, 11th, & 12th Grades (Payment Plan = Down Payment + $50.00 monthly payment)
TEXT COSTS	Included in tuition
TIME LIMITS	Minimum 5 weeks / Maximum 12 weeks / 4 years to complete program
TRANSFER HOURS	Yes: up to 75% of graduate credits
CURRICULUM	Automotive (2 courses) Building (3) Business (8) Drafting (1) English (19) Foreign Languages (4) Hobby Courses (4) Home Living (6) Mathematics (7) Science (7) Social Studies (7)
COMMENTS	EXCELLENT tuition rates, particularly with text costs included. Good catalog and materials, and bi-monthly newsletter for students. School is a non-profit distance learning institution. Over three million students since founding: 200,000 since 1946. $21,000.00 in annual graduate scholarship awards for continuing post-secondary education.

Brigham Young University Indepedent Study

206 Harman Continuing Education Building
Provo UT 84602-2868
800-914-8913 / 801-422-2868
www.byu.edu/webapp/home/index.jsp

Catalog Info	2007-2008
Accreditation	Northwest Association Commission on Accreditation
Diploma	Yes: Adult Diploma Program* (24 Carnegie Units)
College Co-Credits	Yes
Tuition	$120.00 per 1/2 Carnegie Unit (ER: $120.00)
Text Costs	Listed / with full bibliography including ISBN#'s
Time Limits	Maximum 1 year / 3 month extension @ $20.00
Transfer Hours	Yes / Students must pass Utah Competency Exam
Curriculum	Accounting (1 course) Art (9) Business Education (8) Career & Technology Education (8) Character Education (6) Communications (1) Computer Science (7) Computers Word Processing (2) Family & Consumer Science (14) Financial Literacy (1) Foreign Languages: American Sign Language (1) Chinese (4) English as a Second Language (2) French (4) German (4) Japanese (4) Latin (4) Russian (4) Spanish (6) Health (8) Humanities (2) Language Arts-English (12) Language Arts-Literature (4) Language Arts-Reading (4) Language Arts-Writing (4) Life Skills (8) Mathematics (15) Music (2) Physical Education (11) Science-Biological (6) Science-Chemistry (4) Science-Earth Systems (5) Science-Physics (5) Social Science-Contemporary Issues (11) Social Science-History/Government (16) Social Science-Self-Guidance (7)
Comments	GOOD tuition rates. Expansive curriculum. Extensive offerings in: Art, Technology, Family & Consumer Sciences, Foreign Languages (unique ASL, Chinese, Japanese, Russian), English & Language Arts, Mathematics, Physical Education, Sciences & Social Sciences.
	*Upon completion a diploma will be issued from an affiliated school district.

Continental Academy

3241 Executive Way, Miramar FL 33025
800-285-3514
www.continentalacademy.com

Catalog Info	2007 – 2008
Accreditation	Southern Association of Colleges & Schools / Commission on International & Trans-Regional Accreditation / National Association for the Legal Support of Alternative Schools
Diploma	Yes
College Co-Credits	No
Tuition	$395.00 for full program (ER: Unknown)
Time Limits	Not Listed
Transfer Hours	Not Listed
Curriculum	Not Listed
Comments	Can't beat the price, but can't evaluate either. An accredited school, but not nearly enough information within initial contact material to evaluate further. School reports that nearly 500 graduates in 2005 went on to higher levels of education based on their diploma.

Griggs International Academy

P.O. Box 437 Silver Spring MD 20914-4437
800-782-4769 / 310-680-6570
www.griggs.edu

Catalog Info	2007 (since 1907)
Accreditation	Middle States Association of Colleges & Schools; Southern Association of Colleges & Schools; Distance Education & Training Council
Diploma	YES: Basic (21-Carnegie Units); College Preparatory (24-Carnegie Units)
College Co-Credits	YES
Tuition	$196.00 (ER: $196.00); $75.00 Placement test fee
Time Limits	Maximum 12-months / 12-month extension @ $25.00
Transfer Hours	YES
Curriculum	Business & Secretarial (3) English (7) Fine Arts (2) Health & Home Economics (4) History (4) Languages: French (1) Spanish (3) Mathematics (7) Religion (5) Sciences (5)
Comments	ABOVE AVERAGE tuition rates. Good catalog. Extensive Elementary & Middle School course offerings. Book buy-back programs.

Hadley School for the Blind

700 Elm Street, Winnetka IL 60093-2554
800-323-4238 / 847-441-8111 (TTY)
www.hadley-school.org

Catalog Info	2006-2008
Accreditation	Distance Education & Training Counsel (1958) / Commission on Accreditation & School Improvement (1978) / Commission on International & Trans-Regional Accreditation
Diploma	Yes (16 Carnegie Units)
College Co-Credits	No
Tuition	Free – For individuals 14-older who are visually impaired
Text Costs	Free
Time Limits	Varies – Minimum: at least one lesson per month
Transfer Hours	Yes – As many credits as a student has
Curriculum	Art (1 course) English (10 courses) Mathematics (5 courses) Social Studies (9 courses) College Preparation (3 courses) Braille (12 courses) Communications (3 courses) Technology (5 courses) Business and Careers (6 courses) Independent Living (23 courses) Language (2 courses) Recreation (10 courses) Diagnostics (6 courses)
Comments	GREAT! tuition rates if one qualifies. Good large print catalog. Incarcerated students & excellent option for systems to create a cost-efficient high school program for visually impaired prisoners. Also Adult, Family, & Professional education training program courses available; see the school listing in the Vocational section).

Indiana University High School

Owen Hall 001 709 East Kirkwood Ave. Bloomington IN 47405-7101
800-334-1011 / 812-855-2292
www.indiana.edu

Catalog Info	2007-2008 (Since 1925)
Accreditation	North Central Association of Colleges & Schools Commission on International & Trans-Regional Accreditation
Diploma	Yes: Standard (40 credits)*; Honors Diploma (47 credits)*
College Co-Credits	YES: 60+ courses through university
Tuition	$66.25 per 0.5 credit/ $132.50 per 1-credit (ER: $197.50); $146.06 dual credit per credit/ $65.00 per course fee/ $40.00 Application fee/ $60.00 Life Experience Portfolio per activity/ $7.00 Learning Portfolio Assesment per section/ $25.00 Iowa Tests of Educational Development per test section
Time Limits	Maximum 12-months / Two 6-month extensions at no cost
Transfer Hours	Up to 35 credits / Learning Portfolio / Life Experience
Curriculum	Art (3 courses) Business Technology Education (6) English (29) Half-Credit English (7) Family & Consumer Services (6) Health Education (1) Mathematics (15) Multidisciplinary Education (2) Science (8) Social Studies (12) World Languages: French (4) German (4) Latin (2) Spanish (6) DUAL-CREDIT COURSES: Anthropology (2 courses) Astronomy (3) Biology (1) Business (2) Classical Studies (3) Communication & Culture (2) Comparative Literature (2) Computer Science (1) Education (1) English (5) Fine Arts (2) Folklore & Ethnomusicology (2) French (2) Geography (2) Geological Sciences (3) Health, Physical Education & Recreation (1) History (5) Linguistics (1) Mathematics (5) Music (2) Philosophy (4) Physics (3) Political Science (2) Psychological & Brain Sciences (2) Religious Studies (1) Sociology (2) Spanish (2)
Comments	ABOVE AVERAGE tuition rates. First rate program; very good catalog. Probably best holistic H.S. diploma opportunity via distance education. Extensive offerings in: English, Mathematics, & Social Sciences.

*1 credit = 0.5 Carnegie Unit

Keystone National High School

920 Central Road, Bloomsburg PA 17815
800-255-4937 / 570-784-5220
www.keystonehighschool.com

Catalog Info	2007 (since 1974)
Accreditation	Distance Education & Training Council / Northwest Association of Accredited Schools
Diploma	YES: (21 credits)*
College Co-Credits	Advanced Placement courses but available only via online instruction
Tuition	$279.00 per credit (ER: $279.00) [includes all textbooks & materials] (Tuition Payment plan available)
Time Limits	Maximum 9 months
Transfer Hours	Yes
Curriculum	Language Arts (8 courses) Mathematics (13) Science (8) Social Sciences (8) Health (2) Fine Arts (2) Electives (2) Spanish (2)
Comments	HIGH tuition rate. Good catalog. Extensive offerings in: Mathematics. Graduates have been accepted at 140+ colleges and universities. "CEO Scholarship Program" awarded to enrolled students. Contact school for details.

*Equal to Carnegie Units

North Dakota Center for Distance Education

1510 12th Avenue North, P.O. Box 5036, Fargo ND 58105-5036
701-231-6000
www.ndisonline.org

Catalog Info	2007-2008
Accreditation	North Central Association Commission on Accreditation Commission on International & Trans-regional Accreditation
Diploma	Yes: $30 Diploma Application fee (21 Carnegie Units)
College Co-Credits	Yes / Credit by Life Experience program
Tuition	Resident: $95.00 per 1/2 Carnegie unit (ER: $118.00) Nonresident: $103.00 per 1/2 Carnegie unit (ER: $126.00) $23.00 per course handling fee
Text Costs	Listed with full bibliography / Avg. $60.00 per course / Used textbook program / Buy-back program 50% of price
Time Limits	Maximum: 1 year / 1 year extension @ $30.00 fee
Transfer Hours	Yes
Curriculum	Agriculture (4 courses) Art (10) Business Education (8) Driver Education (1) English (17) Family & Consumer Science (5) Mathematics (15) Music (4) Physical Education & Health (5) Science (15) Social Studies (17) Technical Education (5) World Languages: French (4) German (4) Latin (4) Spanish (6) Advanced Placement Courses: Calculus (2) English (2) History (2)
Comments	GOOD Tuition rates. Good informative catalog. Honor Roll program. Two scholarship programs that prisoners may qualify for. Contact the "Scholarship Team" for applications.

Stratford Career Institute

P.O. Box 875, Champlain NY 12919-0875
800-363-0058
www.scitraining.com

Catalog Info	2007
Accreditation	"SCI's High School Diploma program is a general studies program and is not intended to be a substitute for state-sponsored GED programs."
Diploma	YES
College Co-Credits	NO
Tuition	$789.00 [All materials included]
Text Costs	(Tuition payment plan available)
Time Limits	Varies – Maximum: 2 years
Transfer Hours	Non-Applicable
Curriculum	"The subjects of instruction are Social Science, English, History, Mathematics, Science, Civics. Emphasis is always on practical, useful applications. For example, the math module covers banking, rotating, and managing one's personal finances as well as algebra and geometry."
Comments	Impossible to evaluate tuition rate. Scanty catalog materials. Questionable if this diploma would be accepted elsewhere.

Texas Tech University
Division of Outreach & Distance Education
Box 42191, Lubbock TX 79409-2191
800-692-6877 / 806-742-7200
www.ode.ttu.edu

Catalog Info	2007 – 2008
Accreditation	Southern Association of Colleges & Schools / Texas Tech University Independent School District / Accredited by the Texas Education Agency
Diploma	Yes: College Pre Plan (24 Carnegie Units)
College Co-Credits	Yes (at college tuition rates)
Tuition	$95.00 per 1/2 Carnegie Unit + $30.00 per course fee (ER: $125.00)
Text Costs	Not Listed / Course bibliography included
Time Limits	6 months / 6 month extension @ $50.00
Transfer Hours	Not Listed
Curriculum	Accounting (2 courses) Business Computer Information Systems (2) Business Image Management & Media (2) Business Law (2) Introduction to Business (2) Keyboarding (1) Recordkeeping (2) Economics (1) English (9) Journalism (2) Family and Consumer Science (2) Art (6) Health Education (1) French (4) Latin (4) Spanish (6) Mathematics (10) Physical Education (3) Science (8) Social Studies (9) Technology Applications (6)
Comments	AVERAGE tuition rates. Good catalog. Extensive program available to the correspondent-student. Extensive offerings in Elementary & Middle School courses.

University of Alabama
Division of Academic Outreach
College of Continuing Studies

Box 870388, Tuscaloosa AL 35487-0388
800-452-5971 / 205-348-9278
www.ua.edu

Catalog Info	2007
Accreditation	Southern Association of Colleges & Schools
Diploma	No
College Co-Credits	No
Tuition	$111.00 + $25.00 registration fee (ER: $136.00)
Time Limits	Minimum 9-weeks / Maximum 12-months / One 30-day extension @ $30.00
Transfer Hours	Non-Applicable
Curriculum	Business Education (4 courses) English (8) Etiquette (1) French (2) German (4) Health Education (2) Humanities (1) Latin (4) Mathematics (11) Personal Development (2) Psychology (1) Science (10) Social Studies (10) Spanish (4) Speech (2)
Comments	AVERAGE tuition rate. Adequate catalog. Extensive offerings in Mathematics, Science & Social Studies.

University of Arizona
Independent Study through Correspondence
Office of Continuing Education & Outreach

P.O. Box 210158, Tuscon AZ 85721-0158
800-772-7480 / 520-626-5667
www.arizona.edu

Catalog Info	2007-2008
Accreditation	North Central Association Commission of Accreditation
Diploma	No
College Co-Credits	No
Tuition	$125.00 per 1/2 Carnegie Unit / $15 course fee (ER: $140.00)
Text Costs	Listed (new & used) / with full bibliography
Time Limits	Maximum 9 months / 3 month extension @ $35.00
Transfer Hours	Non-Applicable
Curriculum	Accounting (2 courses) Art (3) Business (5) Computer Science (1) English (22) Family & Consumer Resources (5) French (4) Geography (2) Government (6) Health (1) History (12) Journalism (1) Latin (4) Law (1) Marketing (1) Mathematics (12) Mexican-American Studies (2) Sciences (14) Social Studies (6) Vocational Courses (2)
Comments	AVERAGE tuition rates. Good catalog. Extensive offerings in: English, History, Mathematics & Sciences.

University of Idaho
Independent Study

P.O. Box 443225, Moscow ID 83844-3225
877-464-3246 / 208-885-3225
www.uihome.uidaho.edu

Catalog Info	2007
Accreditation	Northwest Association Commission on Accreditation
Diploma	No
College Co-Credits	No
Tuition	$90.00 per 1/2 Carnegie Unit / $25.00 course fee (ER: $148.33)
Text Costs	Listed
Time Limits	Maximum 1 year / 6-month extension @$35.00
Transfer Hours	Non-Applicable
Curriculum	Consumer Economics (1 course) Mathematics (2) Science (2) Social Studies (2)
Comments	GOOD tuition rates. Good catalog.

University of Missouri
Center for Distance Education & Independent Study

136 Clark Hall, Columbia MO 65211-4200
800-609-3727 / 573-882-2491
www.missouri.edu

Catalog Info	2007
Accreditation	North Central Association Commission on Accreditation
Diploma	Yes: General High School or College Prepatory
College Co-Credits	Yes: "Dual Enrollment Program" permits students to enroll in college-level courses @ 50% of standard tuition rates
Tuition	$140.00 per 1/2 Carnegie Unit / $20.00 course fee (ER: $160.00)
Text Costs	Listed with full bibliography
Time Limits	Maximum 9 months / Minimum 30 days / 3-month extension: $30.00
Transfer Hours	Yes
Curriculum	Business (10 courses) Family & Consumer Sciences (4) Fine Arts (3) Foreign Languages: French (2) German (5) Japanese (1) Latin (4) Spanish (6) / Language Arts (11) Mathematics (10)
Comments	ABOVE AVERAGE tuition rates. Good catalog. Note: By taking courses from this school you will be supporting a bloated penal system. The state legislature has financed the 8th largest per capita incarceration rate by proportionally decreasing allocations from the higher education budget (necessitating inflated tuitions) and shifting the funding to the penal system. Thus, every time someone pays tuition, they are inadvertently supporting the incarceration of a prisoner. It's your choice, but there are plenty of other options to choose from.

University of Nebraska–Lincoln
Extended Education & Outreach
Independent Study High School

900 North 22nd Street, P.O. Box 888400, Lincoln NE 68588-8400
866-700-4747 / 402-472-2175
www.unl.edu

Catalog Info	2007-2008
Accreditation	North Central Association Commission on Accreditation Nebraska / Department of Education
Diploma	Yes (20 Carnegie Units)
College Co-Credits	Yes
Tuition	$140.00 per 1/2 Carnegie Unit (ER $185.00)
Text Costs	Listed / Title & ISBN#s / Syllabus $10-$20
Time Limits	Maximum 1 year / 3-month extension @ $35.00
Transfer Hours	Yes: up to 5 Carnegie Units per academic year enrolled
Curriculum	Business & Consumer Mathematics (2 courses) Mathematics (3 courses) Music Theory (1 course) French (2 courses) Spanish (2 courses)
Comments	ABOVE AVERAGE tuition rates. Good catalog. Majority of courses are online. Honor Roll program. Potential scholarship opportunity. Contact school for application; deadline October 31st with awards issued in November.

University of Nevada, Reno
Independent Learning
Extended Studies

P.O. Box 14429, Reno NV 89507
800-233-8928 / 775-784-4652
www.unr.edu/content

Catalog Info	2007-2008
Accreditation	Commission on Colleges of the Northwest Association / Approved by the Nevada State Board of Education
Diploma	No
College Co-Credits	Yes / dual credits must be approved by diploma issuer
Tuition	$100.00 per 1/2 Carnegie Unit / Stationery, Handling, & Syllabus fees $50.00 per course
Text Costs	Listed with full bibliography / Avg. $70.00 per course
Time Limits	Maximum 1 year / Minimum 6 weeks / 6-month extension @ $75.00
Transfer Hours	Non-Applicable
Curriculum	English (8 courses) Health (1 course) History (4 courses) Life Skills (1 course) Mathematics (4 courses) Science (6 courses)
Comments	AVERAGE tuition rates. Good informative catalog.

University of Oklahoma
Center for Independent & Distance Learning

1600 Jenkins Avenue, Room 101, Norman OK 73072-6507
800-942-5702/ 405-325-1921
www.ou.edu/web/home.html

Catalog Info	2007-2008 (Since 1913)
Accreditation	North Central Association Commission on Accreditation / Commission on International & Trans-regional Accreditation
Diploma	YES
College Co-Credits	YES: 125 undergraduate courses available
Tuition	Not Listed
Time Limits	Minimum 6 weeks / Maximum 9 months / 1 extension @ s40
Transfer Hours	Yes if from accredited institution
Curriculum	Business Education (4 courses) Computer Technology (3) Family & Consumer Sciences (5) Fine Arts (5) Music (1) Foreign Languages: French (4) German (6) Latin (4) Spanish (4) / Health (1) Language Arts – English (18) Journalism & Mass Communication (2) Vocabulary (2) Mathematics (12) Personal Development: Peer Counseling (2) Study Skills (1) / Science: Aviation (1) Biology (2) Chemistry (2) General Science (2) Geology (2) Meteorology (1) Physical Science (2) Physics (2)/ Social Studies: Economics (1) Geography (1) Government (3) History (13) Native American Studies (2) / Psychology (1) Sociology (1)
Comments	Shiny, wholly inadequate, fold-out brochure. No way to effectively evaluate or advise regarding this program. More detailed info should be available with follow-up letter with specific questions, but that shouldn't be necessary when making an initial program inquiry.

University of Wisconsin
Independent Study

505 South Rosa Road Suite 200, Madison WI 53719-1277
877-895-3276 / 608-262-2011
www.wisc.edu

Catalog Info	2007-2008
Accreditation	North Central Association Commission on Accreditation
Diploma	None
College Co-Credits	No
Tuition	$125.00 per 1/2 Carnegie unit / $50 course fee (ER: $175.00)
Text Costs	Bibliography listed
Time Limits	Maximum: 12 months / 3-month extension @$25.00
Transfer Hours	Non-Applicable
Curriculum	Art (1 course) Biology (2) Business (2) English (2) French (2) German (4) Health (1) Latin (2) Mathematics (2) Music (2) Polish (2) Russian (8) Spanish (4) Study Skills (1)
Comments	ABOVE AVERAGE tuition rates. Good catalog.

Vocational Program Outlines

Adams State College
Extended Studies

208 Edgemont Boulevard, Alamosa CO 81102
800-548-6679 / 719-587-7671
www.adams.edu

Program	Victim Advocacy Certificate
Founded	Unknown
Accreditation	North Central Association of Colleges & Schools
Tuition	$525 (ER: $525.00)
Text Costs	Not Listed / Bibliography
Time Limits	Maximum 1 year / Minimum 6 weeks
Curriculum	Session 1: Legal Terminology & Process, Theories of Victimization, Effects on Victims & Guidelines for Response. Review Crime Victims Statutes. Session 2: Crisis Theories & Intervention, Response, Understanding & Nature of Crisis. Assesment of Situation & Implementation of Effective Listening Skills to Determine Best Support System. Session 3: Facts & Myths of Domestic Violence, Crimes Against Children, Sexual Assault & Related Crimes. Restraining Orders, Police Procedures, Guidlines for Assisting Murder Victim Survivors & Role of Victim Advocate. Job Search Strategies & Placement Possibilities.
Description	Participants will be prepared to work in victim advocacy areas, such as domestic violence shelters, crisis centers & hotlines, and with government agencies to assist victim processing through the justice system toward successful recovery.
Comments	FAIR tuition rate. VHS, DVD or audio delivery options beyond print. Take the course, adopt the curriculum & teach the program at your prison. Imagine presenting this certificate to the parole board. How I would love to be the proverbial "fly on the wall" to hear how they dismiss your restorative justice efforts then.

Adams State College
Extended Studies

208 Edgemont Boulevard, Alamosa CO 81102
800-548-6679 / 719-587-7671
www.adams.edu

Program	Alternative Dispute Resolution Certificate
Founded	Unknown
Accreditation	North Central Association of Colleges & Schools
Tuition	$525 (ER: $525.00)
Text Costs	Not Listed / Bibliography
Time Limits	Maximum 1 year / Minimum 6 weeks
Curriculum	Session 1: Intro History & Origin of Adr-mediation / Session 2: Techniques for Adr, Mediation Process & Role of the Mediator / Session 3: Business Disputes, Settlement Issues in the Business Sector, Employment Disputes & Employer/employee Relationships. Job Search Strategies & Placement Possibilites.
Description	Course is designed to train and qualify students to develop or participate in conflict mediation processes. Focuses on both traditional and non-traditional dispute resolution options. Course is geared for all professionals focused on "interest-based bargaining."
Comments	FAIR tuition rate. VHS, DVD or audio delivery options beyond print. An open industry and one suited to those who have an affinity for negotiations and ability to perceive "both sides" of an issue.

American Bible Academy
Prison Outreach International

P.O. Box 1490, Joplin MO 64802
417-781-9100
www.arm.org/aba.htm

Program	Certificates of Completion (Bible Study)
Founded	Unknown (Catalog: Current)
Accreditation	No
Tuition	Free to Prisoners & Spouses
Text Costs	Free / 120-page soft-cover textbooks
Time Limits	Maximum / Not Listed
Curriculum	#001 Gospel of John (3 exams) / #102-1 Christian Doctrine Vol. I (3 exams) / #102-2 Christian Doctrine Vol. II (3 exams); #002-1 Book of Acts Vol. I (3 exams) / #002-2 Book of Acts Vol. II (3 exams) / #104 Gospel of Mark (3 exams) / #105 Galatians & Philippians (3 exams)
Description	Each course comes with a textbook/workbook written by respected Bible College Professors & Christian Educators. These courses are more advanced than many studies offered at no cost to prisoners. A certificate of completion is awarded for each course with at least a 70% average on exams.
Comments	OUTSTANDING tuition rates!! Inmate and spouse scholarship program specifically designed to support the bond between husband and wife in their mutual spiritual journey by sharing the same educational enlightenment. First six courses also available in Spanish.

American Institute of Applied Science

100 Hunter Place, Youngsville NC 27596
800-354-5134 / 919-554-2500
www.aiasinc.com

Program — Forensic Science Program 101

Founded — 1916

Accreditation — Distance Education & Training Council

Tuition — $859.00 + (774.00) + (10% discount for full payment at enrollment) (Installment 6/12 month payment plans available) (ER: $184.00)

Text Costs — Materials included with tuition.

Time Limits — No specific limit / Minimum four lessons per month

Curriculum — 101C Criminal Investigation ($230.00)* 101M Modus Operandi ($87.00)* 101FI Firearms Identification ($230.00)* 101Q Questioned Document Examination ($189.00)* 101P Police Photography ($230.00)* 101F Fingerprint Classification & Identification ($558.00)* 101FR Fingerprint Recording & Latent Print Development ($277.00)*

Description — This program is designed to provide a fundamental background in forensic science to law enforcement professionals and others who wish to pursue a career in criminal investigation. GED minimal prerequisite.

Comments — GOOD tuition rates. Program 101 transferable to Burlington County College (which has a long history with prisoner-students) for 6 accredited credit hours ($774.00 tuition + $330.00 registration fees = $1104 / 6 credits = $184.00 per hour). Incarcerated students currently enrolled; student needs to advise school regarding particular instutional packaging/materials rules. Request letter from facility stating it will accept school's materials. Excellent course of study for paralegals and those aspiring to investigation. Also good for those analyzing their own cases for "expert witness" error. Good and descriptive catalog. Over 350 law enforcement agencies throughout the world accept or require these forensic programs.

*(Individual Course Costs)

American Institute of Applied Science

100 Hunter Place, Youngsville NC 27596
800-354-5134 / 919-554-2500
www.aiasinc.com

Program	Forensic Science Program 201
Founded	1916
Accreditation	Distance Education & Training Council
Tuition	$365.00 +($329.00) (ER: $170.00) + (10% discount for full payment at enrollment) (Installment 6/12 month payment plans available) (ER: $170.00)
Text Costs	Materials included with tuition.
Time Limits	No specific limit / Minimum four lessons per month
Curriculum	201F Fundamentals of Forensic Investigation ($128.00)* 210T Trace Evidence & Its Significance ($107.00)* 201A Fundamentals of Arson & Explosion Investigations ($107.00)* 201B Significance of Blood in Criminal Investigations ($87.00)* 201D Forensic Investigations into Drugs & Alcohol ($128.00)*
Description	This program is designed especially for students who have completed Program 101 and for law enforcement professionals who have a background in forensic applications. It allows the student to gain a greater understanding of the processes involved in forensic investigations and selected forensic laboratory techniques. GED minimal prerequisite.
Comments	GOOD tuition rates. Program 201 transferable to Burlington County College (which has a long history with prisoner-students) for 3 accredited credit hours ($329.00 tuition + $180.00 registration fees = $170.00 per hour). Incarcerated students currently enrolled; student needs to advise school regarding particular instutional packaging/materials rules. Requests letter from facility stating it will accept school's materials. Excellent course of study for paralegals and those aspiring to investigation. Also good for those analyzing their own cases for "expert witness" error. Good and descriptive catalog. Over 350 law enforcement agencies throughout the world accept or require these forensic programs. *(Individual Course Costs)

Brigham Young University
Independent Study

120 Morris Center, Provo UT 84602-1514
800-914-8931 / 801-422-2868
www.byu.edu

Program	Personal Enrichment Courses
Founded	1978
Accreditation	Northwest Association of Colleges & Schools
Tuition	$28.00 per course
Text Costs	Listed with full bibliography, but most courses do not have additional books beyond standard inclusive materials
Time Limits	Maximum 1 year / 3-month extension @ $20.00
Curriculum	Computer Science (1 course) Computers-Word Processing (2) Family History/Geneology-Introductory (2) Family Life (1) Family Life-Family Education (2) Family Life-Parenting (2) Gardening (2) Peoples & Cultures (1) Personal & Family Finance (3) Personal Development (1) Reading (1) Religion- LDS Temples (2) Religion-Teachings of the Living Prophets (1) Religion-The Joseph Smith Translation (2) Religion-The New Testament (7) Religion-The Old Testament (1) Sciences (2) Spelling (3) Writing (3)
Description	Various, well-designed personal enrichment courses covering numerous subjects, but predominantly courses on religion from the Mormon viewpoint.
Comments	GOOD pricing. Respectable school & program. Informative catalog. Interesting subjects.

Catholic Distance University

120 East Colonial Highway, Hamilton VA 20158
888-254-4CDU- / 540-388-2700

Program	Advanced Catechist Certificates (11 courses)
Founded	1983 (2007 – 2008)
Accreditation	Distance Education & Training Council / NCEA
Tuition	$135.00 per course
Text Costs	Does not exceed $15.00 per course. Actual cost may be less since books often used in multiple courses. The Catechism of the Catholic Church & RSV Bible, Catholic Edition required for all courses. Some courses require $30.00 video tape supplements.
Time Limits	4 months / Extensions unknown / 4 years to complete certificate program
Curriculum	Theology (5 courses) Catechetical Methods (2 courses) Scripture (2 courses) Electives (2 courses)
Description	Upon completion of two programs students should be able to: (1) Teach the essential and fundamental content of Catholic Doctrine, (2) Use Sacred Scripture for Catechesis, (3) Apply the foundations of Catholic morality within catechesis, (4) Identify appropriate catechetical principles and methods for faithful catechesis, and (5) Provide a catechesis that reflects the proper relationship of prayer and doctrinal truths with daily living.
Comments	GOOD tuition rates for CEU credits. Incarcarated students. Highly focused.

Religious Resources for Catholic Prisoners: Catholic Information Services, Knights of Columbus, Box 1971, New Haven CT 06509. The Knights offer a ten-lesson study course in Catholic history doctrine. The course is taken two lessons at a time. Those who grade the lessons will answer your questions about the Catholic faith. A certificate is awarded upon satisfactory completion of the course. Information booklets are also available. Contact Fr. John V. McGuire, CSSR.

Catholic Home Study Services, Box 363, Perryville, MO 63775-0383. The Confraternity produces a six-lesson study in book form called "The Kingdom of Christ." The content of the study is done in a question and answer format, which is easy to follow. The course is not complicated but requires serious study to comprehend the essence of its Catholic teachings. Contact Fr. Oscar J. Lukefahr, CM.

TAN Books and Publishers, Inc., Box 424, Rockford, IL 61105. TAN is a major publisher that has established a book distribution program to enrich the faith of incarcerated Catholics through its St. Anthony Mary Claret Mission Program. Many of the books offered are Christian classics and include books rich in Catholic doctrine, history and tradition. Contact Mrs. Anita Mioni.

Cleveland Institute of Electronics

1776 East 17th Street, Cleveland OH 44114-3679
800-243-6446 / 216-781-9400
www.cie-wc.edu

Program	Electronics Technology with Laboratory (33 credits)*
Founded	1934 (as Practical Radio Institute)
Accreditation	Distance Education & Training Council / ACE / CHEA
Tuition	$2,295.00 for entire course (ER: $69.55) (Financing plan option @ 12% with 35 $75.00 payments)
Text Costs	Materials included with tuition
Time Limits	24 months / Extensions upon request
Curriculum	93 Lessons — Current & Voltage / Static Electricity / Ohm's Law / Conductors & Insulators / Parallel Circuits, etc.
Description	Designed for students with no previous electronics experience, providing solid core of instruction in electronics. You will learn about AC & DC current theory, identifying components, working with printed circuit boards, relays, robots, regulated power supplies, and troubleshooting digital systems. Graduates readily employable as electronics technicians. At no extra cost, CIE offers graduates the professional preparation for passage of the Associate Level of the "Certified Electronics Technician" (CET) exam administered by the International Society of Certified Electronics Technicians.
Comments	EXCELLENT tuition rates. Good catalog. Don't know how it is arranged (depending on specific institution's restrictions), but school has many incarcerated students. Solid looking vocational training program. Must work through all clearances at your particular institution before enrollment. Send requests specifically to: Andrew S Podsiadlo, Jr, Guidance Counselor.
	*33 credits applicable to CIE's A.A.S. Electronics Degree Program (See: CIE in College section)

Cleveland Institute of Electronics

1776 East 17th Street, Cleveland OH 44114-3679
800-243-6446 / 216-781-9400
www.cie-wc.edu

Program	Electronics Technology with FCC License Preparation (24 credits)*
Founded	1934 (as Practical Radio Institute)
Accreditation	Distance Education & Training Council / ACE/ CHEA
Tuition	$1,795.00 for entire course (ER: $74.79) (Financing plan option @ 12% with 26 $75.00 payments)
Text Costs	Materials included with tuition
Time Limits	18 months/ Extensions upon request
Curriculum	80 Lessons — Currents & Voltages in AC Currents / Amplifiers / Oscillators/ Robot Control System / Modern Modulation Methods / Digital & Data Communication, Transmitters, etc.
Description	Course prepares students to obtain the General Radiotelephone Operator License (GROL) and gain a thorough education in electronics. The GROL is required to adjust, maintain, or internally repair any FCC licensed radiotelephone transmitters in the aviation, maritime and international fixed public radio services. It is issued for the lifetime of the holder. At no extra cost, CTE offers graduates the professional preparation for passage of the GROL and FCC exams.
Comments	EXCELLENT tuition rates. Good catalog. Don't know how it is arranged (depending on specific institution's restrictions), but school has many incarcerated students. Solid looking vocational training program. Must work through all clearances at your particular institution before enrollment. Send requests specifically to: Andrew S Podsiadlo Jr, Guidance Counselor.

*24 credits applicable to CIE's A.A.S. Electronics program (SEE: CIE in College section)

Cleveland Institute of Electronics

1776 East 17th Street, Cleveland OH 44114-3679
800-243-6446 / 216-781-9400
www.cie-wc.edu

Program	Broadcast Engineering (23 credits)*
Founded	1934 (as Practical Radio Institute)
Accreditation	Distance Education & Training Council / ACE/ CHEA
Tuition	$1,795.00 for entire course (ER: $78.04) (financing plan option @ 12% with 26 $75.00 payments)
Text Costs	Materials included with tuition
Time Limits	24 months / Extensions upon request
Curriculum	95 Lessons: Resonant Circuits/ Radio Frequency Amplifiers/ Telemetry/ Antennas & Wave Guides/ Camera Chains & Synchronizing Generators/ Circuit Analysis, etc.
Description	Course prepares student with specialized knowledge required for a career as a broadcast engineering technician at an AM or FM radio station or at a TV station. Course is also valuable for the cable television technician who must maintain or repair and maintain studio equipment. Course explores important theories and principles related specifically to broadcasting, but because it does not contain any laboratory work, it is best suited for students who already have some previous education or practical experience in electronics. Graduates may be eligible to earn Certified Broadcast Technologist certification (CBT) from the Society of Broadcast engineers (SBE), which is the only organization devoted to the advancement of all levels and types of broadcast engineers.
Comments	EXCELLENT tuition rates. Good catalog. Don't know how it is arranged (depending on specific institution's restrictions), but school has many incarcerated students. Solid looking vocational training program. Must work through all clearances at your particular institution before enrollment. Send requests specifically to: Andrew S Podsiadlo, Jr, Guidance Counselor.

*23 credits applicable to CIE's A.A.S. Electronics program (SEE: CIE in College section)

Cleveland Institute of Electronics

1776 East 17th Street, Cleveland OH 44114-3679
800-243-6446 / 216-781-9400
www.cie-wc.edu

Program	Industrial Electronics with PLC Technology (23 credits)*
Founded	1934 (as Practical Radio Institute)
Accreditation	Distance Education & Training Council / ACE / CHEA
Tuition	$1,745.00 for entire course (ER: $75.86) (financing plan option @ 12% with 26 $75.00 payments)
Text Costs	Materials included with tuition
Time Limits	18 months / Extensions upon request
Curriculum	78 lessons: Simplifying Circuit Analysis by using Kirchoff's Laws / Using Semiconductor Diodes / Unregulated Power Supplies / Operation of Tubes & Transistors / Understanding & Using the Occilloscope / Digital Switching Units / Logic Circuit Tracing by Using Boolean Algebra, etc.
Description	Course prepares student with a thorough understanding of industrial electronics and essential troubleshooting techniques necessary to maintain, repair and program a wide array of industrial electronic equipment including robotics, servos and programmable logic contollers. In addition, students graduate with the ability to read and understand many different types of schematics and operational manuals. Course provides a well-rounded electronics education, but because it does not contain laboratory work, it is best suited for those students who already have some previous education or practical experience in electronics. At no additional cost, CIE offers graduates the professional preparation necessary to pass the Associate Level of the Certified Electronics Technician (CET) Exam administrated by the International Society of Certified Electronics Technicians (ISCENT).
Comments	EXCELLENT tuition rates. Good catalog. Don't know how it is arranged (depending on specific institution's restrictions), but school has many incarcerated students. Solid looking vocational training program. Must work through all clearances at your particular institution before enrollment. Send requests specifically to: Andrew S Podsiadlo, Jr, Guidance Counselor.
	*23 credits applicable to CIE's A.A.S. Electronics program (SEE: CIE in College section)

Prisoners' Guerrilla Handbook

Cleveland Institute of Electronics

1776 East 17th Street, Cleveland OH 44114-3679
800-243-6446 / 216-781-9400
www.cie-wc.edu

Program	Electronics Engineering (70 credits)
Founded	1934 (as Practical Radio Institute)
Accreditation	Distance Education & Training Council / ACE / CHEA
Tuition	$3,285.00 for entire course (ER: $46.92) (financing plan option @ 12% with 56 $75.00 payments)
Text Costs	Materials included with tuition
Time Limits	30 months / Extensions upon request
Curriculum	89 Lessons: Solving Linear Equations / Pulse Processing Circuits / Network Theorems / Steady-State Circuits / Diode Networks/ Practical Matrix Theory for Engineers / Natural Logarithims / Operational Amplifiers / Angle Modulation Transmission, etc.
Description	Course is an advanced level program designed for technicians and engineers who want a deeper understanding of electronic circuits and advanced mathematics. Prerequisites are a high school diploma or GED with at least one year of algebra or geometry, or the completion of any CIE course, an in-depth working experience in the field of electronics, or the permission of CIE's Director of Instruction. At no additional cost, CIE offers graduates the professional preparation necessary to pass the Associate Level of the Certified Electronics Technician (CET) Exam administrated by the International Society of Certified Electronics Technicians (ISCENT).
Comments	EXCELLENT tuition rates. Good catalog. Don't know how it is arranged (depending on specific institution's restrictions), but school has many incarcerated students. Solid looking vocational training program. Must work through all clearances at your particular institution before enrollment. Send requests specifically to: Andrew S. Podsiadlo, Jr, Guidance Counselor.
	*70 credits applicable to CIE's A.A.S. Electronics program (SEE: CIE in College section)

Cleveland Institute of Electronics

1776 East 17th Street, Cleveland OH 44114-3679
800-243-6446 / 216-781-9400
www.cie-wc.edu

Program	Electronics Technology & Advanced Troubleshooting (38 credits)*
Founded	1934 (as Practical Radio Institute)
Accreditation	Distance Education & Training Council / ACE / CHEA
Tuition	$3,945.00 for entire course (ER: $103.81) (financing plan option @ 12% with 73 $75.00 payments)
Text Costs	Materials included with tuition
Time Limits	36 months / Extensions upon request
Curriculum	118 Lessons: Intro to Television / Video Circuits & the CRT/ Color Symptom Troubleshooting / Interpreting Oscilloscope Waveforms / Modern Equipment Construction, etc.
Description	Course expands upon the Electronics Technology with Laboratory program to include electronics troubleshooting training. Students graduate with ability to service consumer electronics such as TV and home audio equipment. At no additional cost, CIE offers graduates the professional preparation necessary to pass the Associate Level of the Certified Electronics Technician (CET) Exam administered by the International Society of Certified Electronics Technicians (ISCENT).
Comments	EXCELLENT tuition rates considering materials are included. Good catalog. Don't know how it is arranged (depending on specific institution's restrictions), but school has many incarcerated students. Solid looking vocational training program. Must work through all clearances at your particular institution before enrollment. Send requests specifically to: Andrew S Podsiadlo Jr, Guidance Counselor.

*38 credits applicable to CIE's A.A.S. Electronics program (SEE: CIE in College section)

Cleveland Institute of Electronics

1776 East 17th Street, Cleveland OH 44114-3679
800-243-6446 / 216-781-9400
www.cie-wc.edu

Program	Electronics Technology with Digital & Microprocessor Laboratories (53 credits)*
Founded	1934 (as Practical Radio Institute)
Accreditation	Distance Education & Training Council / ACE / CHEA
Tuition	$4,495.00 for entire course (ER: $84.81) (financing plan option @ 12% with 90 $75.00 payments)
Text Costs	Materials included (This laboratory-intensive course contains all the lessons and equipment described in the Electronics Technology with Laboratory program plus NEW lessons on PIC technology.)
Time Limits	42 months / Extensions upon request
Curriculum	155 Lessons: AC & DC Circuit Theory / Relays & Robots / Regulated Power Supplies / Troubleshooting Digital Systems / PIC Program Coding & 68HC11 Microcontroller / Digital Integrated Circuits, etc.
Description	Course is CIE's most advanced troubleshooting program. Course expands on the lessons from the Electronics Technology with Laboratory program to prepare students for jobs in computer maintenance, advanced industrial and microprocessor control. At no additional cost, CIE offers graduates the professional preparation necessary to pass the Associate Level of the Certified Electronics Technician (CET) Exam administered by the International Society of Certified Electronics Technicians (ISCET)
Comments	EXCELLENT tuition rates considering materials are included. Good catalog. Don't know how it is arranged (depending on specific institution's restrictions), but school has many incarcerated students. Solid looking vocational training program. Must work through all clearances at your particular institution before enrollment. Send requests specifically to: Andrew S Podsiadlo Jr, Guidance Counselor. ***You will need access to an oscilloscope to complete this course.

*53 credits applicable to CIE's A.A.S. Electronics program (SEE: CIE in College section)

Cleveland Institute of Electronics

1776 East 17th Street, Cleveland OH 44114-3679
800-243-6446 / 216-781-9400
www.cie-wc.edu

Program	Computer Programming (18 credits)*
Founded	1934 (as Practical Radio Institute)
Accreditation	Distance Education & Training Council / ACE / CHEA
Tuition	$1,795.00 for entire course (ER: $99.72) (financing plan option @ 12% with 26 $75.00 payments)
Text Costs	Materials included with tuition
Time Limits	12 months / Extensions upon request
Curriculum	48 Lessons: Intro to Computers / Applications Software / Finding Files & Data/ Disk Maintenance / Hardware: Input, Processing, Output & Storage Devices/ Software: Systems & Applications Packages / Graphics: On-Line Information & other PC Applications / Designing a Web page / Exploring Arrays & Strings, etc.
Description	Course with lab was designed to provide an individual with little or no background with the knowledge to join the ever-growing field of computer programming. Students graduate with the ability to understand, analyze and program various computer applications used in the business, manufacturing and service industries today. Ability to develop and build web pages and to install and run applications and perform basic system management on PCs also taught.
Comments	EXCELLENT tuition rates considering materials are included. Good catalog. Don't know how it is arranged (depending on specific institution's restrictions), but school has many incarcerated students. Solid looking vocational training program. Must work through all clearances at your particular institution before enrollment. Send requests specifically to: Andrew S. Podsiadlo Jr, Guidance Counselor. ***Requires Windows 98/XP + modem + Microsoft Internet Explorer + Internet connection.
	*18 credits applicable to CIE's A.A.S. Computer program (SEE: CIE in College section)

Cleveland Institute of Electronics

1776 East 17th Street, Cleveland OH 44114-3679
800-243-6446 / 216-781-9400
www.cie-wc.edu

Program	A+ Certification & Computer Technology (18 credits)*
Founded	1934 (as Practical Radio Institute)
Accreditation	Distance Education & Training Council / ACE / CHEA
Tuition	$1,295.00 for entire course (ER: $71.94) (financing plan option @ 12% with 18 $75.00 payments)
Text Costs	Materials included with tuition.
Time Limits	8 months / Extensions upon request
Curriculum	33 Lessons: Section I: Introduction to Computers / Section II: Operating Systems Microsoft Windows / Section III: A+ Certification Preparation
Description	Course created to train students with little or no computer background about computer technology. Students will learn how to troubleshoot PCs while preparing for the CompTIA A+ Certification Exam. Such certification signifies the individual possesses the knowledge and skills needed for an entry level Computer Service Technician. The A+ certification is one of the most desired credentials in the information technology industry, and is sponsored by the Computing Technology Industry Association (CompTIA).
Comments	EXCELLENT tuition rates considering materials are included. Good catalog. Don't know how it is arranged (depending on specific institution's restrictions), but school has many incarcerated students. Solid looking vocational training program. Must work through all clearances at your particular institution before enrollment. Send requests specifically to: Andrew S. Podsiadlo Jr, Guidance Counselor.

*18 credits applicable to CIE's A.A.S. Computer program (SEE: CIE in College section)

Cleveland Institute of Electronics

1776 East 17th Street, Cleveland OH 44114-3679
800-243-6446 / 216-781-9400
www.cie-wc.edu

Program	CompTIA Network + Certification & Computer Technology (15 credits)*
Founded	1934 (as Practical Radio Institute)
Accreditation	Distance Education & Training Council / ACE / CHEA
Tuition	$1,295.00 for entire course (ER: $86.33) (financing plan option @ 12% with 18 $75.00 payments)
Text Costs	Materials included with tuition
Time Limits	8 months / Extensions upon request
Curriculum	30 Lessons: Hands on Training Lab (CD ROM)/ Introduction to Computers/ Operating Systems- Microsoft Windows/ Network+ Certification Preparation
Description	Course created to train students with little or no computer background about computer technology. Students will learn how to troubleshoot PCs while preparing for the CompTIA A+ Certification Exam. Such certification validates competency in networking administration and support. Those holding Network+ Certification demonstrate critical knowledge of media and topologies, protocols and standards, network implementation and network support.
Comments	EXCELLENT tuition rates considering materials are included. Good catalog. Don't know how it is arranged (depending on specific institution's restrictions), but school has many incarcerated students. Solid looking vocational training program. Must work through all clearances at your particular institution before enrollment. Send requests specifically to: Andrew S. Podsiadlo Jr, Guidance Counselor. *15 credits applicable to CIE's A.A.S. Computer program (SEE: CIE in College section)

Cleveland Institute of Electronics

1776 East 17th Street, Cleveland OH 44114-3679
800-243-6446 / 216-781-9400
www.cie-wc.edu

Program	Introduction to Computers & Microsoft Office (9 credits)*
Founded	1934 (as Practical Radio Institute)
Accreditation	Distance Education & Training Council / ACE / CHEA
Tuition	$1,245.00 for entire course (ER: $138.33) (financing plan option @ 12% with 18 $75.00 payments)
Text Costs	Materials included with tuition
Time Limits	8 months / Extensions upon request
Curriculum	30 Lessons: Computer Hardware, Software Fundamentals / Microsoft Windows XP / Microsoft Word / Microsoft Excel / Microsoft Access / Microsoft Power Point/ Printers & Fonts / Maintaining Computers / Graphics / Internet
Description	Course created to train students with little or no computer background how to run and maintain a PC and be proficient with Microsoft Office. Step-by-step learning labs cover real world projects in Excel, Word, Access & Power Point.
Comments	VERY GOOD tuition rates considering materials are included. Good catalog. Don't know how it is arranged (depending on specific institution's restrictions), but school has many incarcerated students. Solid looking vocational training program. Must work through all clearances at your particular institution before enrollment. Send requests specifically to: Andrew S Podsiadlo Jr, Guidance Counselor.

*9 credits applicable to CIE's A.A.S. Computer program (SEE: CIE in College section)

Cleveland Institute of Electronics

1776 East 17th Street, Cleveland OH 44114-3679
800-243-6446 / 216-781-9400
www.cie-wc.edu

Program	Introduction to Home Automation Installation (9 credits)*
Founded	1934 (as Practical Radio Institute)
Accreditation	Distance Education & Training Council / ACE / CHEA
Tuition	$1,245.00 for entire course (ER: $138.33) (financing plan option @ 12% with 18 $75.00 payments)
Text Costs	Materials included with tuition
Time Limits	8 months / Extensions upon request
Curriculum	30 Lessons: Structured Wiring / Home Computer Networks / Troubleshooting Audio & Video Systems / Home Lighting Systems / Telecommunications/ HVAC & Water Management / Security Systems / Computer Hardware / Software Fundamentals
Description	Course does not require any previous home networking experience but by the end of the course student will have a solid foundation in home technology integration. Course instructs how to install, service and troubleshoot home automated systems such as home security, audio/video, computer networks, electrical wiring, HVAC, cable and satellite while preparing for the HTI+ and CEDIA installer certifications.
Comments	VERY GOOD tuition rates considering materials are included. Good catalog. Don't know how it is arranged (depending on specific institution's restrictions), but school has many incarcerated students. Solid looking vocational training program. Must work through all clearances at your particular institution before enrollment. Send requests specifically to: Andrew S. Podsiadlo Jr, Guidance Counselor.

*9 credits applicable to CIE's A.A.S. Computer program (SEE: CIE in College section)

Cleveland Institute of Electronics

1776 East 17th Street, Cleveland OH 44114-3679
800-243-6446 / 216-781-9400
www.cie-wc.edu

Program	Wireless & Electronic Communications (17 credits)*
Founded	1934 (as Practical Radio Institute)
Accreditation	Distance Education & Training Council / ACE / CHEA
Tuition	$1,795.00 for entire course (ER: $105.58) (financing plan option @ 12% with 26 $75.00 payments)
Text Costs	Materials included with tuition.
Time Limits	24 months / Extensions upon request
Curriculum	84 Lessons: Using Semiconductor Diodes / Radio Frequency Amplifiers / Microwave Communications Systems / Transmission Lines & Wave Guides / Lasers in Communications & Industry / Infrared / Bluetooth / Digital Cellular Phones, etc.
Description	Course designed to provide a thorough understanding of wireless and personal communications along with providing a solid core of instructions in electronics. Courses explore important theories and principles related specifically to communications, but because it does not contain any laboratory work, it is best suited to those students who already have some previous education or practical experience in electronics. At no cost course prepares student for CET and FCC exams. The Associate Level of the Certified Technical Exam (CET) is administered by the International Society of Certified Electronics Technicians (ISCET).
Comments	VERY GOOD tuition rates considering materials are included. Good catalog. Don't know how it is arranged (depending on specific institution's restrictions), but school has many incarcerated students. Solid looking vocational training program. Must work through all clearances at your particular institution before enrollment. Send requests specifically to: Andrew S Podsiadlo Jr, Guidance Counselor.

*17 credits applicable to CIE's A.A.S. Electronics degree program (SEE: CIE in College section)

Cornell Lab of Ornithology Home Study Course

159 Sapsucker Woods Road, Ithaca NY 14850-1999
800-843-2473 / 607-254-2473
www.birds.cornell.edu

Program	Certificate of Completion in Bird Biology
Founded	Unknown
Accreditation	Unknown
Tuition	$299.50 includes all materials
Text Costs	($99.50) 1300 page textbook included in course price
Time Limits	Non-Applicable
Curriculum	Birds & Humans: A Historical Perspective / World of Birds / A Guide to Bird Watching / Form and Function: The External Bird / What's Inside: Anatomy & Physiology / Birds on the move: Flight and Migration / Evolution of Birds & Avian Flight / Understanding Bird Behavior / Vocal Behavior / Nests, Eggs & Young: Breeding Biology of Birds / Individuals, Populations & Communities: The Ecology of Birds / Birds Conservation
Description	Learn about bird behavior, ecology, conservation, and many other subjects. This comprehensive course was written by twelve leading ornithologists, edited by Lab of Ornithology staff, and illustrated by acclaimed wildlife artist John Schmitt. The course is written at the introductory college level, but is suitable for anyone with an inquiring mind and a serious interest in birds. It introduces important biological concepts by exploring the major topics in ornithology. Current and past students include bird watchers of all skill levels as well as high school and college students, professional biologists, wildlife rehabilitators, and homeschoolers.
Comments	Impossible to evaluate tuition rates. Adequate program brochure. Audio CD included in materials. If interested in subject matter, this looks like a well-prepared course from a top-notch university affiliated program.

Global University: Berean School of the Bible

1211 South Glenstone, Avenue Springfield MO 65804
800-443-1083 / 417-862-9533
www.globaluniversity.edu

Program	Certificates: Certified Minister (54 CEUs) New Licensed Minister (60 CEUs) Transitional Licensed Minister (40 CEUs) New Ordained Minister (48 CEUs) Old Ordained Minister (56 CEUs)
Founded	1967 (Catalog: 3rd Quarter 2007)
Accreditation	Distance Education & Training Council
Tuition	FREE to Prisoners / $10.00 per course S & H fee
Text Costs	25% Prisoner Discount / Listed in Brochure
Time Limits	Maximum 18 months / $10.00 reactivation fee / Prisoner-student allowed two simultaneous enrollments
Curriculum	Varies per certificate requirement but outlined in Prisoner Course Order Form: Bible (16 courses) Christian Service (18) General Education (4) Ministry / Practical Theology (23) Theology / History (9)
Description	Upon completion of the Ministerial Studies Diploma (including Certified, Licensed & Ordained), the student will have met the minimum academic requirements to apply for the ordination process with the General Council of the Assemblies of God in the United States. The student will have mastered basic Bible content (Old & New Testaments), theological principles, and practical ministry skills for service in a church leadership position. Individuals who serve churches other than AG may substitute the organization specific courses with courses from non AG ministerial courses to complete curriculums.
Comments	OUTSTANDING tuition rates! Good catalog & materials, plus specific counselor assigned to prisoner-students. If you question your ability to handle college level work, try a few courses from this program to evaluate your actual abilities. Can't beat the cost! Courses also available in Spanish.
	Note: Continuing Education Units (CEUs) are a nationally recognized standard by the education community to measure participation in learning activities; these units cannot be equated with college credits.

Graduate School
USDA Self-Paced Training

P.O. Box 25605 Denver CO 80225-0605
888-744-GRAD
www.grad.usda.gov

Program	Certificate of Accomplishment for each course completed
Founded	1921
Accreditation	American Council on Education College Credit Recommendation Service
Tuition	$125.00- $355.00 for varying CEU credits
Text Costs	Not Listed / Many courses include material in tuition costs
Time Limits	Maximum 6 months / 6-month extension @ $50.00
Curriculum	Accounting (1 course) English & Writing (8) Human Resource Management (8) Management & Supervision (7) Project Management (3)
Description	Well-designed courses of varying skill-improvement subject matter.
Comments	GOOD pricing. Good catalog. Incarcerated students. Offers college-level credit courses and certificate programs (see school in college section).

Hadley School for the Blind

700 Elm Street, Winnetka IL 60093
800-323-4238 / 847-446-8111 (TTY)
www.hadley-school.org

Program	Adult Continuing Education Program
Founded	1920
Accreditation	Distance Education & Training Council (1958) / Commission on Accreditation & School Improvement (1978) / Commission on International & Trans-Regional Accreditation (2003)
Tuition	FREE for adults who are blind or visually impaired
Text Costs	Free
Time Limits	Varies — Minimum at least one lesson per month
Curriculum	Art (1 course) English (10) Mathematics (5) Science (4) Social Studies (9) College Preparation (3) Braille (12) Communication (3) Technology (5) Business & Careers (6) Independent Living (22) Language (2) Recreation (10) Diagnostics (6)
Description	The Adult Continuing Education Program offers a variety of courses for adults who are blind or visually impared that covers areas ranging from braille and academic studies to independent living, life adjustment, technology and recreation.
Comments	GREAT tuition rates if one qualifies. Good large print catalog. Incarcerated students & excellent option for systems to create a cost-efficient training program for visually impaired prisoners. Adult Continuing Education courses. See lisiting in High School section for FREE diploma program. CEUs available.

Hadley School for the Blind

700 Elm Street, Winnetka IL 60093
800-323-4238 / 847-446-8111 (TTY)
www.hadley-school.org

Program	Family Education Program
Founded	1920
Accreditation	Distance Education & Training Council (1958) / Commission on Accreditation & School Improvement (1978) / Commission on International & Trans-Regional Accreditation (2003)
Tuition	FREE for parents, grandparents, spouses, children or siblings of severely visually impaired adults
Text Costs	Free
Time Limits	Varies — Minimum at least one lesson per month
Curriculum	Early Childhood & Elementary Years (9 courses) Braille (4) Independent Living (14) Diagnostics (1)
Description	The Family Education courses offer topics of interest to parents of blind children and family members of blind adults. Topics include child development, independent living and braille instruction.
Comments	GREAT tuition rates if one qualifies. Good large print catalog. Incarcerated students & excellent option for systems to create a cost-efficient training program for visually impaired prisoners. Adult Continuing Education courses. See listing in High School section for FREE diploma program. CEUs available.

Hadley School for the Blind
700 Elm Street, Winnetka IL 60093
800-323-4238 / 847-446-8111 (TTY)
www.hadley-school.org

Program	Professional Education Program
Founded	1920
Accreditation	Distance Education & Training Council (1958) / Commission on Accreditation & School Improvement (1978) / Commission on International & Trans-Regional Accreditation (2003)
Tuition	FREE: Professionals, volunteers, or service providers who currently work with visually impaired individuals and who can understand English at a high school level.
Text Costs	Free
Time Limits	Varies — Minimum at least one lesson per month
Curriculum	Braille (4 courses) Early Childhood & Elementary Years (6) Technology (2) Independent Living (14) Additional Studies (1) Diagnostics (2)
Description	Professional Education features courses for professionals, volunteers and service providers who work with blind people. Designed to help students sharpen existing skills or aquire new ones in independent living, low-vision, and braille.
Comments	GREAT tuition rates if one qualifies. Good large print catalog. Incarcerated students & excellent option for systems to create a cost-efficient training program for prisoners or larger community via transcription & narration services, such as that provided by the Center for Braille & Narration Production at the Jefferson City Correctional Center, Missouri. See listing in High School section for FREE diploma program. CEUs available.

Institute of Logistical Management

315 West Broad Street / P.O. Box 427, Burlington NJ 08016
888-ILM-4600 / 609-747-1515
www.logistics-edu.com

Program	Certified Logistics Practitioner (48 credits)*
Founded	1923 (Oldest logistics distance learning school in the world)
Accreditation	Distance Education & Training Council / ACE / CHEA / Council of Supply Chain Management Professional Association
Tuition	$695.00 per course (ER: $231.66)/ $75.00 one time application fee
Text Costs	$175.00 per course / If text repeated, $50.00 fee only
Time Limits	6 months / Extensions upon request
Curriculum	Fundamentals of Transportation & Logistics / Transportation System / Transportation Management / Business Logistics Principles / Business Logistics Systems Analysis / Warehousing Management / Global Logistics Management/ Freight Claims Management/ Hazardous Materials Compliance / Motor Carrier Operations / Law I – Rail & Motor Carrier / Law II- Ocean, Air & International / Export Management / Import Management / Information Technology in Supply Chain & Logistics Part One / Inventory Management
Description	These transportation and logistics courses are "real world" and not about theory. When students complete this work they will be very knowledgeable in the practical application of this logistics education for their careers.
Comments	AVERAGE tuition rates; expensive materials. Not very informative materials.

*ILM is currently evaluating offering an Associate Degree in Logistics & Supply Chain. Will "Grandfather" all students & require 15 credits of additional General Education Courses.

*ILM cannot guarantee particular colleges will accept all credit recommendations, but the University of Phoenix accepts these courses, and other leading schools accept them into their Business Degree programs. |

Moody Bible Institute
Moody Distance Learning Center
820 North LaSalle Blvd., Chicago IL 60610
800-758-6352

Program	Scofield Courses: BI 808 – Old Testament (9 CEUs) BI 898 – New Testament (9 CEUs) TH 897 – Biblical Doctrine (9 CEUs) 7825 – Plus Three Adult Courses (3 CEUs) 3403 Scofield Complete (27 CEUs) 7850 Shofield Plus Three (12 CEUs)
Founded	1901 (2007 – 2008)
Accreditation	Higher Learning Commission of the North Central Association / Association for Biblical Higher Education
Tuition	$90.00 to $585.00 per program / $60.00 savings per packet order off individual courses.
Text Costs	Included with course materials
Time Limits	6 months per course / 48 months per certificate program
Curriculum	BI 808 – 2-volume overview of the Word. Learn the principles for interpreting Scriptures and Bible Study techniques. / BI 898 – 2-volume study of the life of Christ, experiences in the early church, the Epistles & Revelation. Also inductive Bible Study methods. / BI 897 – 2-volume study of key theological issues of sanctification, justification, atonement, etc., and study of major Biblical doctrinal teachings of the end times. / 782 – Packages of Biblical basis of Missions, Successful Soul Winning & Teaching with Results. / 3403 – Package of Old Testament, New Testament & Bible Doctrine. / 7850 Package of Old Testament, New Testament, & Bible Doctrine, Biblical Basis of Missions, Successful Soul Winning & Teaching with Results
Description	See above.
Comments	GOOD rates. Minimally informative catalog, but adequate enough for initial evaluation. If seeking more in-depth biblical education this program is worth investigating.

Moody Bible Institute
Moody Distance Learning Center

820 North LaSalle Blvd., Chicago IL 60610
800-758-6352

Program	Biblical Studies Certificate (10 CEUs) / New Testament Studies Certificate (10 CEUs) / Old Testament Studies Certificate (10 CEUs) / Personal Ministry & Leadership Certificate (10 CEUs)
Founded	1991 (2007 – 2008)
Accreditation	Higher Learning Commission of the North Central Association / Association for Biblical Higher Education
Tuition	$49.00 per Continuing Education Unit (CEU) / $367.50 per 10-course certificate program (package deal)
Text Costs	Included with course materials
Time Limits	6 months per course / 48 months per certificate program
Curriculum	Biblical Information (25 courses) Education (6 courses) Evangelical (2 courses) Theology (7 courses)
Description	Detailed Biblical/Theological education as defined by this school. Contact school for catalog with more detailed description.
Comments	GOOD rates. Minimally informative catalog, but adequate enough for initial evaluation. If seeking more in-depth biblical education this program is worth investigating.

National Tax Training School

P.O. Box 767, Mahwah NJ 07430-0767
800-914-8138 / 201-684-0828
www.nattax.com

Program	Tax Consultant Certificate / Higher Course in Federal Taxation
Founded	1952 (updated for 2007 tax law)
Accreditation	Distance Education & Training Council
Tuition	$595.00 or payment plan of $305.00 @ enrollment & $305.00 after 45 days
Text Costs	All materials included in tuition
Time Limits	Minimum 8 weeks / Maximum 1 year
Curriculum	INDIVIDUALS: Introduction, Determination of Taxation, Gross Income Inclusions & Exclusions, Property Transactions – Capital Gains & Losses, Deductions & Losses, Itemized Deductions, Losses & Bad Debts, Employee Expenses & Deferred Compensation, Depreciation, Cost Recovery, Depletion, Amortization & Inventory Costs, Accounting Periods & Methods, Property Transactions, Nontaxable Exchanges & Section 1231 & Recapture, Special Tax Computation Methods, Payment of Tax & Tax Credits. CORPORATIONS: Tax Research, Corporate Formations & Capital, Structure, Corporate Income Tax, Corporate Non-Liquidating Distributions, Corporate Tax Levies, Corporate Acquisitions & Reorganizations, Partnership Formation & Operation, Special Partnership Issues, S Corporations, Gift Tax, Estate Tax, Income Taxation of Trusts & Estates, Administrative Procedures. TABLES & FORMS: Tax Table & Rate Schedules, Tax Research Working Paper File, Completed Tax forms, MACRS & ACRS Tables, SRTPs, Comparison of Tax Attributes for C & S Corporations & Partnerships, Credit for State Death Taxes, Actuarial Tables.
Description	For those with experience in the tax field, this advanced training course in partnerships, corporations and fiduciaries will prepare you for the IRS Special Enrollment Examination. Approved for CPE Credit for CPAs and Enrolled Agents.
Comments	More than 25,000 graduates, many incarcerated students. Each student assigned a specific counselor. Tax preparation business open to ex-cons; only CA & OR have licensing standards. Business is stable (there are always taxes to file), can be operated full or part-time, hourly rates above minimum wage, operated with no overhead. Latest IRS special enrollment examination included with copy of solutions for study. SPECIAL BONUS: Building and Operating a Profitable Tax Practice manual and three-year guidance and updating service and business consultation.

National Tax Training School

P.O. Box 767, Mahwah NJ 07430-0767
800-914-8138 / 201-264-0828
www.nattax.com

Program	Certificate of Graduation / Federal Tax Course
Founded	1952 (updated for 2007 tax law)
Accreditation	Distance Education & Training Council
Tuition	$645 / Payment plan of 3 installments of $230.00
Text Costs	All materials included in tuition
Time Limits	Minimum 8 weeks / Maximum 1 year
Curriculum	20 lessons especially developed for home study, using language that is understood even by students without an accounting background. Program is designed to impart the knowledge needed to understand the theory and concepts of US federal tax systems in addition to practical application of filing tax forms.
Description	If you have no previous knowledge of tax preparation the Federal Tax Course will provide you with the proper training, covering all pertinent phases of the Federal individual income tax so you can become a professional tax preparer.
Comments	More than 25,000 graduates, many incarcerated students. Each student assigned a specific counselor. Tax preparation business open to ex-cons; only CA & OR have licensing standards. Business is stable (there are always taxes to file), can be operated full or part-time, hourly rates above minimum wage, operated with no overhead. Hey, remember the cell block seasonal business in the "Shawshank Redemption" :+)
	SPECIAL BONUS: Building and Operating a Profitable Tax Practice manual and three-year guidance and updating service and business consultation.

Rhodec International

59 Coddington Street, Suite 104, Quincy MA 02169
617-472-4942
www.rhodec.edu

Program	Associate Diploma in Interior Design (One Year)
Founded	1960
Accreditation	Distance Education & Training Council
Tuition	Unknown
Text Costs	Unknown
Time Limits	Maximum 1 year / Extensions (possible with extra fees)
Curriculum	12 LESSONS -- Elements & Principles of Design / Detailed Color Theory, including full Development of Color Schemes; Materials such as Wood, Stone, Metal, Glass, etc. / How to Present Sample Boards / Measuring Rooms & Estimating Materials Quantities / Simple Plans & Elevations / Decorative Paint Finishes / Planning Rooms / Soft Furnishings – Textiles, Window Treatments, Upholstery, Carpets / Internal Fittings / Lighting / Making the Most of Your Time when You Visit Exhibitions / Professional Practice
Description	This program is a thorough introduction to the subject. The grounding in the topic will be more than sufficient to enable you to take on small commissions and advise family and friends.
Comments	Unable to evaluate tuition rates; though director will consider discounts for prisoners on case-by-case basis. Good catalog materials, though lacking pricing. Incarcerated students. Very specialized program in field wide open to ex-felons. Graduates and/or students are eligible for membership in the following professional associations: American Society of Interior Designers, National Council for Interior Design Qualification, International Interior Design Assocation. New students will receive inducement packet of books, materials, and association memberships in value of more than $300.00.

Rhodec International

59 Coddington Street, Suite 104 Quincy MA 02169
617-472-4942
www.rhodec.edu

Program	Diploma in Interior Design (60 credits)
Founded	1960
Accreditation	Distance Education & Training Council
Tuition	Unknown
Text Costs	Unknown
Time Limits	Maximum 3 years / Extensions (possible with extra fees)
Curriculum	Materials (6 credits) History of Interior Design (6 credits) Drafting for the Interior Designer (6 credits) Design (3 credits) Color (6 credits) Furniture & Fittings, I (6 credits) Furniture & Fittings, II (6 credits) Construction of Interiors (6 credits) Professional Practice (3 credits) Final Test (12 credits)
Description	The program trains the student to know, understand and put into practice the prime essentials of successful interior design as a professional. The school's course curriculum has been created by leading designers and educators, custom writing all materials (no "off the shelf" textbooks), fulfilling as close to possible the educational criteria recommended by professional and educational organizations involved in the subject.
Comments	Unable to evaluate tuition rates; though director will consider discounts for prisoners on case-by-case basis. Good catalog materials, though lacking pricing. Incarcerated students. Very specialized program in field wide open to ex-felons. Above average students may qualify for Diplomas with "Merit" or with "Distinction" based on the quality of their work. Graduates and/or students are eligible for membership in the following professional associations: American Society of Interior Designers, National Council for Interior Design Qualification, International Interior Design Association. New students will receive inducement packet of books, materials, and association memberships in value of more than $300.00.

Seminary Extension

901 Commerce Street Suite 500, Nashville TN 37203
800-229-4612 / 615-242-2453
www.seminaryextension.org

Program	Certificates in Biblical Backgrounds, Church Leadership, Pastoral Training (6 courses) Certificate in Discipleship Studies (10 courses) Certificate of Merit (10 courses)
Founded	1951
Accreditation	Distance Education & Training Council
Tuition	$39.00 per course / $30 admin fee & $22 S&H (ER: 91.00)
Text Costs	Listed
Time Limits	Maximum 6 months / 6-month extension
Curriculum	Bible (3 courses) Old Testament (9) New Testament (23) Theology (4) Church History (5) World Religions (2) Christian Ethics (2) Pastoral Ministries (9) General Ministries (5) Christian Education (1) Religious Education (6) Church Administration (1) Christian Music (3)
Description	Basic level courses are for the purpose of helping ministers in the very practical areas of Christian ministry. Students who prefer easy to read materials will find these courses especially helpful. These are also beneficial for persons for whom English is not their first language.
Comments	FAIR tuition rates. Informative catalog but can be confusing. Incarcerated students. College-level (ACE) courses available (see college section). Courses available in Spanish.

SJM Family Foundation, Inc

P.O. Box 167365, Irving TX 75016
972-636-5257
www.prisonerresources.com

Program	Non Profit Management & Grantsmanship (15 CEUs)
Founded	2007 (as National Social Rehabilitation & Re-Entry Program)
Accreditation	Certified Fundraising Executives International (2008) (formerly: Association of Fundraising Professionals & Healthcare Philanthropy)
Tuition	$100.00 (will accept checks, money orders & stamps!) Payment plan: $35.00 down payment / $5.50 installments. Indigent inmates may receive one chapter every 60 days
Text Costs	Inside Nonprofit Organizations (638 pages) (included)
Time Limits	Non-Applicable
Curriculum	Intro to Nonprofits / Board Development & Relations / Conflict Resolution / Strategic Planning / Internal Employee Communication / Nonprofit Ethics / Public relations / Nonprofit Program Mgt / Program Planning / Marketing to Nonprofits / Grantwriting 101 / Media Buying / Media Relations / Basics of Publicity Writing / Foundation & Corporate Grants / Federal & State Grants / Web Finding Sources for Grantwriters, Researchers, and Nonprofit Orgs / Writing the Effective Letter of Support / Evaluation Techniques in Grantwriting / Literary Grants & Fellowships / Creating Budgets / National Institute of Health Major Grants / Writing Styles in Grant Development / Mgt of Grant Budget / Acquisition of Small Grants for Nonprofit Orgs / Preparation of Budget proposals / A21: An Office of Mgt & Budget Circular for Educational Institutions / Web Based Sources for the Administration of Grant Funds / ABC's of Grant Reviewing
Description	The program is designed for prisoners and ex-offenders who desire a basic understanding of the nonprofit sector and are interested in working for social service agencies, nonprofit organizations, community groups, corporate volunteer programs and prison ministries.
Comments	EXCELLENT tuition rates considering the course is the book & two certificate programs are included. This foundation has worked hard to create and maintain a quality education program for prisoners. The materials used in this course were developed in an ACE course at the Federal Correctional Institute – Danbury in the Fall of 2006. I have personally reviewed these materials and am impressed with the level of training it provides.

Stratford Career Institute

P.O. Box 875, Champlain NY 12919-0875
800-363-0058
www.scitraining.com

Program	Computer Training / Creative Writing / Florist-Floral Design / Home Inspector / Photography / Teacher Aide / Writing Stories for Children
Founded	Unknown
Accreditation	Unknown
Tuition	$539.00 (Tuition Payment Plan available)
Text Costs	All materials included with tuition
Time Limits	Not Listed
Curriculum	Initial contact materials do not include programs' specific curriculums. For more detailed information contact SCI for course specifics.
Description	EXAMPLE – "COMPUTER PROGRAMMING is an introduction to all aspects of computer components and operations. It explores fundamental concepts in Windows and detailed training in software packages that are most commonly used in the office environment. The course includes software for word processing, spreadsheets, and business presentation."
Comments	Unable to evaluate tuition rates. Minimal initial catalog materials. May be satisfying skill developing programs. Students will have to research and evaluate for themselves. Could well provide options with which to develop greater depth in particular interests.

Stratford Career Institute

P.O. Box 875, Champlain NY 12919-0875
800-363-0058
www.scitraining.com

Program	Astrology / Parapsychology / Gardening & Landscaping / Internet Specialist / Sewing & Dressmaking
Founded	Unknown
Accreditation	Unknown
Tuition	$479.00 (Tuition Payment Plan available)
Text Costs	All materials included with tuition
Time Limits	Not listed
Curriculum	Initial contact materials do not include programs' specific curriculums. For more detailed information contact SCI for course specifics.
Description	EXAMPLE — "ASTROLOGY/PARAPSYCHOLOGY is a comprehensive program for anyone interested in the predictive sciences. The course provides a serious and in-depth study of the most fascinating elements of parapsychology, astrology, palmistry, numerology and the I Ching."
Comments	Unable to evaluate tuition rates. Minimal initial catalog materials. May be satisfying skill developing programs. Students will have to research and evaluate for themselves. Could well provide options with which to develop greater depth in particular interests.

Stratford Career Institute

P.O. Box 875, Champlain NY 12919-0875
800-363-0058
www.scitraining.com

Program Accounting / Art / Bookkeeping / Child Day Care Management / Child Psychology / Drug & Alcohol Counseling / Early Childhood Education / Fashion Merchandising & Design / Fitness & Nutrition / Locksmith / Motorcycle-ATV Repair / Private Investigator / Real Estate Appraiser / Security-Police Sciences / Start Your Own Business / Travel & Tourism / Wedding Consultant

Founded Unknown

Accreditation Unknown

Tuition $579.00 (Tuition Payment Plan available)

Text Costs All materials included with tuition

Time Limits Not listed

Curriculum Initial contact materials do not include programs' specific curriculums. For more detailed information contact SCI for course specifics.

Description EXAMPLE: "ACCOUNTING — instructs students in a broad range of manual and computerized accounting functions, such as maintaining ledgers and journals, creating balance sheets and financial statements, controlling cash, and preparing payroll. Special procedures for end-of-fiscal-period work, proprietorships, partnerships and corporations are also covered, as well as tasks related to forming and dissolving business organizations."

Comments Unable to evaluate tuition rates. Minimal initial catalog materials. May be satisfying skill developing programs. Students will have to research and evaluate for themselves. Could well provide options with which to develop greater depth in particular interests.

Stratford Career Institute

P.O. Box 875, Champlain NY 12919-0875
800-363-0058
www.scitraining.com

Program	Administrative Assistant – Secretary / Auto Mechanics / Conservation – Environmental Sciences / Cooking & Catering / Criminal Justice / Electrician / English as a Second Language / Medical Office Assistant / Pharmacy Assistant
Founded	Unknown
Accreditation	Unknown
Tuition	$639.00 (Tuition Payment Plan available)
Text Costs	All materials included with tuition
Time Limits	Not Listed
Curriculum	Initial contact materials do not include programs' specific curriculums. For more detailed information contact SCI for course specifics.
Description	EXAMPLE: "ADMINISTRATIVE ASSISTANT – SECRETARY prepares you for the role of the administrative assistant in the modern working environment. You will be trained in secretarial procedures for the automated office. Lessons on administrative support services cover topics such as assisting at conferences, banking and record keeping."
Comments	Unable to evaluate tuition rates. Minimal initial catalog materials. May be satisfying skill developing programs. Each student will have to research and evaluate for themselves. Could well provide options with which to develop greater depth in particular interests.

Stratford Career Institute

P.O. Box 875, Champlain NY 12919-0875
800-363-0058
www.scitraining.com

Program	Business Management / Cosmotology – Esthetics / Dental Assistant / Funeral Service Education / Interior Decorating / PC Repair / Psychology – Social Work / Relaxation Therapist / Small Engine Repair / Veterinary Assistant
Founded	Unknown
Accreditation	Unknown
Tuition	$679.00 (Tuition Payment Plan available)
Text Costs	All materials included with tuition
Time Limits	Not Listed
Curriculum	Initial contact materials do not include programs' specific curriculums. For more detailed information contact SCI for course specifics.
Description	EXAMPLE: "BUSINESS MANAGEMENT focuses on the latest perspectives with such critical topics as business organization and systems, human resources management, marketing and finance, statistics and data management, business law, labor relations, international business, the securities market and computers."
Comments	Unable to evaluate tuition rates. Minimal initial catalog materials. May be satisfying skill developing programs. Each student will have to research and evaluate for themselves. Could well provide options with which to develop greater depth in particular interests.

Stratford Career Institute

P.O. Box 875, Champlain NY 12919-0875
800-363-0058
www.scitraining.com

Program	Computer Programming / Contractor – Construction Management / Desktop Publishing & Design / Forensic Science / Hotel & Restaurant Management / Medical Transcriptionist / Physical Therapy Aide
Founded	Unknown
Accreditation	Unknown
Tuition	$739.00 (Tuition Payment Plan available)
Text Costs	All materials included with tuition
Time Limits	Not Listed
Curriculum	Initial contact materials do not include programs' specific curriculums. For more detailed information contact SCI for course specifics.
Description	EXAMPLE: "FORENSIC SCIENCE is a fascinating program covering everything from processing the crime scene to the fundamentals of DNA analysis, and handwriting and document examinations. This is a rewarding career field where the love of science can be applied to the good of society, public health and safety."
Comments	Unable to evaluate tuition rates. Minimal initial catalog materials. May be satisfying skill developing programs. Each student will have to research and evaluate for themselves. Could well provide options with which to develop greater depth in particular interests.

Stratford Career Institute

P.O. Box 875, Champlain NY 12919-0875
800-363-0058
www.scitraining.com

Program	Medical Billing Specialist
Founded	Unknown
Accreditation	Unknown
Tuition	$789.00 (Tuition Payment Plan available)
Text Costs	All materials included with tuition
Time Limits	Not Listed
Curriculum	Initial contact materials do not include programs' specific curriculums. For more detailed information contact SCI for course specifics.
Description	MEDICAL BILLING SPECIALIST program provides you with a knowledge of medical terminology. The basics of insurance billing and coding are covered. Procedured coding and types of claims are also presented in depth. Types of insurance plans are surveyed and presented as well.
Comments	Unable to evaluate tuition rates. Minimal initial catalog materials. May be satisfying skill developing programs. Students will have to research and evaluate for themselves. Could well provide options with which to develop greater depth in particular interests.

Stratford Career Institute

P.O. Box 875, Champlain NY 12919-0875
800-363-0058
www.scitraining.com

Program	Drafting with AutoCAD
Founded	Unknown
Accreditation	Unknown
Tuition	$979.00 (Tuition Payment Plan available)
Text Costs	All materials included with tuition
Time Limits	Not Listed
Curriculum	Initial contact materials do not include programs' specific curriculums. For more detailed information contact SCI for course specifics.
Description	DRAFTING WITH AUTOCAD teaches both traditional drafting skills, and Computer Aided Design (CAD) using AutoCAD software, the global standard in CAD software. This program covers topics ranging from drafting equipment and supplies to advanced AutoCAD techniques.
Comments	Unable to evaluate tuition rates. Minimal initial catalog materials. May be satisfying skill developing programs. Students will have to research and evaluate for themselves. Could well provide options with which to develop greater depth in particular interests.

University of Arizona
Independent Study Through Correspondence
Office of Continuing Education & Outreach

P.O. Box 210158, Tucson AZ 85721-0158
520-621-7724 / 800-955-8632
www.arizona.edu

Program	Certificate of Completion
Founded	1915
Accreditation	North Central Association of Colleges & Schools
Tuition	Varies: $45.00- $125.00
Text Costs	Listed (new & used) with full bibliography; some courses no texts
Time Limits	Maximum 1 year / 3-month extension @ $40.00
Curriculum	Learning Calligraphy ($60/ no text) / Ford Mustang 1964 1/2-1973: A Survey of Ford's Original Pony Car ($65/ text $15.50) / English as a Second Language (2 courses) ($125 / audiotape $15.00) / Beginning Conversational Spanish ($109 / no text) / Color Yourself Successful ($45 / no text) / Introduction to Museum Work ($85/ text $22.50) / Job Hunting in Today's Market (under revision) / Creative Writing ($125 / texts $40)
Description	Non-credit courses offer you new and exciting opportunities for growth. For detailed course descriptions access the catalog.
Comments	FAIR pricing. Good catalog. Some interesting & practical courses.

University of Georgia
Certificate Programs
Center for Continuing Education

1197 South Lumpkin Street, Suite 193, Athens GA 30602-3603
800-325-2090
www.uga.edu

Program	Sports Turfgrass Management Certificate Course (14 CEUs)
Founded	Unknown
Accreditation	Southern Association of Colleges & Schools
Tuition	$289.00 members*/ $349.00 non-members (ER: $26.00)
Text Costs	Materials included / $16.00 S&H USA — $75.00 foreign
Time Limits	Maximum 12 months / 3-month extension @ $60.00
Curriculum	1. Turfgrass Growth, Development & Physiology / 2. Turfgrass Characterization, Identification & Adaptation / 3. Basic Soils / 4. Establishment / 5. Fertilization / 6. Mowing / 7. Water Management & Irrigation / 8. Sports Turf Cultivation (Proctored Exam #1 – #8) / 9. Weeds / 10. Insects / 11. Diseases / 12. Pesticides / 13. Sports Field Construction & Renovation / 14. Special Sports Field Management Practices / 15. Diagnosing Common Sports Turf Problems / 16. Turfgrass & Environment (Proctored Exam #9 – #16)
Description	Offers up-to-date information on the establishment and care of sports fields. Whether you are new to the lawn care field or an "old-timer," this course will help you become a safer and more efficient professional. Your customers will notice improvements in service, and you will get more satisfaction out of your work.
Comments	GOOD per CEU tuition. Decent brochure, also a Spanish option with entire course materials. A business wide open to ex-cons. A lot of guys get out and start lawn care businesses. This would give you a step up on the competition.
*Membership in: PLANET, GCSAA & STMA

University of Georgia
Certificate Programs
Center for Continuing Education

1197 South Lumpkin Street, Suite 193, Athens GA 30602-3603
800-325-2090
www.uga.edu

Program	Certification in Turfgrass Management (33 credits)
Founded	Unknown
Accreditation	Southern Association of Colleges & Schools
Tuition	$171.00 (ER: $171.00)
Text Costs	Not Listed
Time Limits	Maximum 9 months / 3-month extension @ $60.00
Curriculum	Introduction to Turfgrass Management CRSS 2830 / Turfgrass Management CRSS 3270 / Turfgrass Management Laboratory CRSS 3270L / Turfgrass Pest Management CRSS /PATH /ENTO / Advanced Turfgrass Science CRSS 4090 / Topics in Crop & Soil Science CRSS 4220 / Turf & Landscape Irrigation Systems APTC 3070 / Horticultural Science HORT 2000 / Landscape Management HORT 4090 / SELECT TWO ELECTIVES FROM: Arts & Sciences, Accounting, Business or Spanish
Description	Rapid advances in turfgrass management technologies and related areas increase the need for education. This certification program offers college-credit courses enabling the student to keep pace with the changing industry.
Comments	GOOD tuition rates. Good catalog, even has section regarding prisoner enrollment (page 6) with certification program (page 44). No admissions tests or transcripts of previous college work required. A field of study wide open to ex-cons, no license requirements.

University of Georgia
Certificate Programs
Center for Continuing Education

1197 South Lumpkin Street, Suite 193, Athens GA 30602-3603
800-325-2090
www.uga.edu

Program	Certified Turfgrass Professional (CTP) (12 CEUs)
Founded	Unknown
Accreditation	Southern Association of Colleges & Schools; Professional Lawncare Network (PLANET)
Tuition	$249.00 members*/ $309.00 non-members (ER: $27.00)
Text Costs	Materials included / $16.00 S&H USA — $75.00 foreign
Time Limits	Maximum 12 months / 3-month extension @ $60.00
Curriculum	1. Turfgrass Growth, Development & Physiology / 2. Turfgrass Characterization, Identification & Adaptation / 3. Soils / 4. Establishment / 5. Fertilization / 6. Mowing / 7. Irrigation (Proctored Exam #1 – #7) 8. Weeds / 9. Insects / 10. Turfgrass Diseases / 11. Pesticides / 12. Turfgrass & Environment / 13. Turfgrass Troubleshooting Construction & Renovation / 14. Customer Relations (Proctored Exam #8 – #14)
Description	Whether you are new to the lawn care field or an "old-timer," this course will help you become a safer and more efficient professional. Your customers will notice improvements in service, and you will get more satisfaction out of your work.
Comments	GOOD per CEU tuition. Decent brochure, also a Spanish option with entire course materials. A business wide open to ex-cons. A lot of guys get out and start lawn care businesses. This would give you a step up on the competition. *Membership in: PLANET, GCSAA & STMA

University of Wisconsin
Independent Study
Disaster Management Center

432 Lake Street, Madison WI 53719
800-462-0876 / 608-262-5441
dmc.engr.wisc.edu

Program	Disaster Management Diploma (60 CEUs)
Founded	1892 (one of the nation's first distance education programs)
Accreditation	North Central Association of Colleges & Schools
Tuition	$125.00 / $145.00 per course (2.0 / 3.5 CEUs) + $80.00 admin fee (ER: $8.00) (Minimum total diploma cost $2,890)
Text Costs	Included with tuition with prepaid S&H
Time Limits	Maximum 12 months / 3-month extension @ $25.00 / 3-months $50.00
Curriculum	Aim & Scope of Disaster Management (2.0 CEUs) / Principles of Management (3.5 CEUs) / Natural Hazards: Causes & Effects (3.0 CEUs) / Disaster Preparedness (2.5 CEUs) / Damage & Needs Assesment (3.0 CEUs) / Disaster Response (3.0 CEUs) / Environmental Health Management after Natural Disaster (2.0 CEUs) / Health Services Organizations in Events of a Disaster (2.5 CEUs) / Emergency Health Management after Natural Disaster (2.0 CEUs) / Epidemiologic Surveillance after Natural Disaster (2.0 CEUs) / Emergency Vector Control after Natural Disaster (2.5 CEUs) / Health Education & Training of Refugee Health Workers (3.0 CEUs) / Disasters & Development (2.5 CEUs)
Description	Comprehensive disaster management encompasses activities in preparedness, predisaster strategies to mitigate a disaster's impact on hazard-prone areas and lessen the loss of life and property. It also includes activities in risk reduction, the longer-term, and large-scale policy decisions that prevent or diminish a disaster's impact. Education and training in all phases of disaster management are key to successful mitigation of impact and effectiveness of response.
Comments	GOOD tuition rates. Good catalog. Interesting program and least expensive and most accessible one identified. Courses in Spanish.

Paralegal Program Outlines

Adams State College Extended Studies

208 Edgemont Boulevard, Alamosa CO 81102
800-548-6679 / 719-587-7671
www.adams.edu

Program	Legal Secretary Certificate Course
Certification	Yes: Certificate of Accomplishment for each course completion
Accreditation	North Central Association of Colleges & Schools
Affiliations	None noted
Tuition	$525.00
Text Costs	Not Listed / Bibliography (text & author) listed (probably will exceed $100.00 in used text costs)
Time Limits	Maximum 12 months / Minimum 6 weeks
Transfer Hours	Non-Applicable
Curriculum	SESSION 1: Introduction to the theory of law, the legal process, and the nature of the practice of law. Discussion will include the process of law as well as specific legal terminology. Ethics are also covered. / SESSION 2: The particulars of law office management and use of technology. Review of actual documents and preparation of some as homework. / SESSION 3: The intricacies of the law office, including office procedure manuals, billing techniques, and overall management. Basics of legal research and proper citation format. Job search strategies and placement possibilities.
Description	This intensive program is designed for beginning and experienced secretaries who are interested in improving their skills and working more efficiently within the law office.
Comments	GOOD tuition rates. Incarcerated students. Good catalog. NOTICE: course can only be taken online, in VHS or audio formats, thus be sure you have access to the selected necessary technologies.

Adams State College
Extended Studies

208 Edgemont Boulevard, Alamosa CO 81102
800-548-6679 / 719-587-7671
www.adams.edu

Program	Paralegal Certificate Course
Certification	Yes: Certificate of Accomplishment for each course completion
Accreditation	North Central Association of Colleges & Schools
Affiliations	None noted
Tuition	$840.00
Text Costs	Not Listed / Bibliography (text & author) listed (probably will exceed $200.00 in used text costs)
Time Limits	Maximum 12 months/ Minimum 6 weeks
Transfer Hours	Non-Applicable
Curriculum	SESSION 1: Legal Terminology, Documents, Ethics and the Litigation Process / SESSION 2: Introduction to the Evidentiary Predicate / SESSION 3: Identifying Relevant Authority / SESSION 4: Introduction to Legal Research / SESSION 5: Legal Research Practice / SESSION 6: Legal Writing and Appellate Procedure"
Description	This intensive, nationally acclaimed program is designed for beginning as well as advanced legal workers. The program offers training in interview techniques, investigation, legal research, document preparation and case preparation for court litigation. The instruction is practice-oriented and relates to those areas of law for which paralegals are in most demand.
Comments	GOOD tuition rates. Incarcerated students. Good catalog. No prerequisites, but a lot of homework. Several jailhouse lawyers reviewed the detailed curriculum and all like this program.

Adams State College
Extended Studies

208 Edgemont Boulevard, Alamosa CO 81102
800-548-6679 / 719-587-7671
www.adams.edu

Program	Legal Investigation Certificate Course
Certification	Yes: Certificate of Accomplishment
Accreditation	North Central Association of Colleges & Schools
Affiliations	None noted
Tuition	$525.00
Text Costs	Not Listed / Bibliography (text & author) listed
Time Limits	Maximum 12 months / Minimum 6 weeks
Transfer Hours	Non-Applicable
Curriculum	Session 1: Intro to legal system, legal & ethical considerations for the investigator, law of agency & coverage of rules of court & evidence. Session 2: General interviewing & investigation techniques, sources of leads & information, fact analysis, taking witness statements, forensic photography, proper service of legal process & surveillance. Session 3: Personal injury investigation techniques, traffic accident reconstruction, premises accidents, employment accidents, government investigation, document analysis & control, financial & equity analysis, testimony & case studies. Job search strategies & placement possibilities.
Description	This program is designed to teach legal investigation to those interested in pursuing a new career and those presently working in the legal field. Graduates will be qualified to work with all types of legal professionals, as well as create their own freelance investigation business.
Comments	GOOD tuition rates. Incarcerated students. Good catalog. No prerequisites, but a lot of homework. Not a bad option for the legal-minded or as an adjunct to paralegal training. Combine your "street smarts" and criminal experience with investigative techniques for a legitimate career.

American Center for Conflict Resolution Institute

5247 Wilson Mills Road #442 Richmond Heights OH 44143
800-517-0857
www.accri.org/programs.html

Program	Paralegal / Legal Assistant (900 clock hours)
Certification	Yes
Accreditation	Approved by the Board of Career Colleges & Schools
Affiliations	Better Business Bureau
Tuition	$1,797.00 (Tuition payment plan available with 0% interest)
Text Costs	All materials included
Time Limits	9 months / 10 lessons take 2-3 weeks
Transfer Hours	Unknown
Curriculum	Paralegal Profession / Law Office Operations / Legal Systems: Understanding Court Structures & Purpose / Legal Research & Terminology / Legal Writing & Analysis / Legal Procedures: Lawsuit Preparation & Maintenance / Legal Subjects I: People Focus / Legal Subjects II: Transaction Oriented / Litigation Alternatives, Conflict Resolution & Negotiation / Getting Paid: Employment, Networking & Future Trends
Comments	HIGH tuition rate. Scanty catalog materials.

American Center for Conflict Resolution Institute

5247 Wilson Mills Road #442, Richmond Heights OH 44143
800-517-0857
www.accri.org/programs.html

Program	Professional Business & Family Mediator (80 clock hours)
Certification	Yes
Accreditation	Approved by the Board of Career Colleges & Schools
Affiliations	Better Business Bureau
Tuition	$899.00 +$24.00 S&H ($999.00 Tuition payment plan available)
Text Costs	All materials included
Time Limits	Minimum 4 months / Maximum 24 months
Transfer Hours	No
Curriculum	Conflict Resolution Overview / Mediation & You / Formal Mediation Process / Legal Considerations in Mediation / Convening Process / Opening Statement / Communication & Information Gathering / Negotiation Stage / Relationship Skills / Problem Solving Skills / Conflict Management Skills / Closing Stage / Ethics / Professional Family Mediation Skills / Professional Business Mediation Skills / Marketing Mediation. Supplements: How to Complete a Memorandum of Understanding – Mediation Settlement Agreement / State Certification, Employment & Marketing Strategies
Comments	Impossible to evaluate tuition rate. Mediocre marketing materials. There are no state requirements/certifications/licenses for the private practice of mediation. Bonus Gifts: "How to Make it Big Resolving Disputes" & "The New Mediator's Kit"

Ashworth College

430 Technology Parkway, Norcross GA 30092
800-640-9524
www.ashworth.college.edu

Founded	1987 (Catalog 2008)
Certification	Associates Degree in Paralegal Studies (60 Credits)
Accreditation	Distance Education & Training Council
Affiliations	
Tuition	$1200.00 for degree program (ER: $20.00) (Payment plan: 24 months @ $49.00 per month)
Text Costs	Included in tuition price
Time Limits	Minimum 6 months / Maximum 4 years / Extensions for fee
Transfer Hours	45 credits / CLEP / DANTES / ACE
Curriculum	First Semester – Intro Business / Business Communication I / Business Law / Intro Paralegalism I / Paralegalism II – Second Semester – Personal Finance / Business Communications II / American Government / Torts / Civil Litigation – Third Semester – Intro Psychology / Criminal Law & Procedure / Real Estate Law / College Mathematics / Law Office Management – Fourth Semester – Intro Computers / Family Law / Legal Research & Writing / Wills, Trusts & Estates / Income Tax Fundamentals
Comments	OUTSTANDING tuition rates, with this caveat: Uncertain how many of these credits will be transferable and/or degree programs accepted by other schools. Poor informational brochure. School claims more than 750,000 graduates worldwide.
	I know of Federal prisoners who have earned degrees from this school, utilizing tuition payment plan, and have been pleased with the quality and used the degrees to obtain post-release employment.

Blackstone Career Institute

P.O. Box 3717, Allentown PA 18106
800-826-9228 / 610-967-3323
www.blackstone.edu

Program	Legal Assistant / Paralegal Program
Certification	Yes: Diploma
Accreditation	Distance Education & Training Council / Middle States Commission on Secondary Schools
Affiliations	National Federation of Paralegal Associates / National Paralegal Association / National Association of Legal Assistants
Tuition	$915.00 (+$132 registration) Payment Plan: $55.00 down payment + 13 payments of $57.50
Text Costs	Course materials included: 14 soft cover, non-metal bindings, texts / 31 lessons / 31 exams totaling 120-pages
Time Limits	Average 12-15 months / Maximum 2 years
Transfer Hours	Yes: evaluated on case-by-case basis
Curriculum	Study packages (SP) compose varying numbers of lessons: SP#1 Law-Its Origin, Nature-Development & Contracts / SP#2 Torts / SP#3 Criminal Law / SP#4 Real Property Part I / SP#5 Real Property Part II / SP#6 Pleadings & Practice in Civil Actions & Criminal Procedure / SP#7 Wills & Trusts / SP#8 Partnerships & Corporations / SP#9 Constitutional Law Part I / SP#10 Constitutional Law Part II / SP#11 Finding, Reading & Using the Law text "Legal Research Study Guide" / SP#12 Legal Research & Writing Study Guide- Finding, Reading & Using the Law / SP#13 Paralegal Career Starter text "How to Find a Job as a Paralegal" Study Guide / SP#14 Ethics for Paralegal Study Unit
Description	Oldest (since 1890) proprietary correspondence paralegal program in the nation. Well-rounded curriculum provides solid legal foundation. Completion of the program qualifies graduates to sit for the Certified Legal Assistant Exam administrated by the National Association of Legal Assistants.
Comments	GOOD tuition rates. Incarcerated students compose one-third of enrollment from over 1000 prisons. Many effective "jailhouse lawyers" have been trained by this school. Info packet includes "Student/Inmate Guide to Enrollment" brochure.

Graduate School
USDA

P.O. Box 25605, Denver CO 80225-0605
888-744-GRAD
www.grad.usda.gov

Founded	1921
Program	Paralegal Study Course
Certification	Yes: Certificate of Accomplishment for each course completion
Accreditation	American Council On Education College Credit Recommendation Service
Affiliations	National Federation of Paralegal Associates / Trial Lawyers of America
Tuition	$355.00 per 3-credit course (ER: $118.33)
Text Costs	Not listed but one or more texts per course required. Contact school for specific course bibliography
Time Limits	Maximum 12 months / 6-month extension @ $50.00
Transfer Hours	Non-Applicable
Curriculum	Administrative Law & Procedure (3 credits)*/ Business Law I (3 credits)*/ The Freedom of Information Act (2 credits)* Intro to Law for Paralegals (3 credits)*/ Legal Ethics (3 credits)*/ Legal Research (3 credits)*/ Legal Writing (3 credits)*
Description	These courses are well designed and have experienced and knowledgeable legal instructors. Courses are primarily paper and pencil workbooks and consist of several lessons, each of which you can usually complete within one to two hours. Each course contains practical exercises and often case studies or reference materials, job aids and audio or video supplements. Courses contain at least one test.
Comments	VERY GOOD tuition rates. Incarcerated students. Good catalog. May be program to accumulate lesser-cost ACE accredited hours for transfer to other diploma/degree granting programs.

*American Council on Education accredited hours. |

Newport University

4101 Westerly Place, Suite #103, Newport Beach CA 92600
949-757-1155
www.newport.edu

Founded	1976 (Catalog 2007 – 2008)
Certification	Juris Doctor ** Bar Preparation (132 units); Juris Doctor** Non-Bar (132 units)
Accreditation	Approved by State of California / Bureau of Private Postsecondary & Vocational Education*
Affiliations	
Tuition	$5,100 annual fee x four years (total $20,400) $100 Application Fee
Text Costs	Not Listed / No bibliography in catalog
Time Limits	Satisfactory progress requires annual curriculum completion per year
Transfer Hours	Up to 99 units / 4th year must be completed @ Newport University
Curriculum	FIRST YEAR- Intro Law / Criminal Law / Contract Law / Tort Law / Criminal Procedure / Legal Analysis, Researching &Writing (34 units) SECOND YEAR- Real Property / Wills & Succession / Trusts / Agency & Partnerships / Remedies / Business Associations (34 units) / THIRD YEAR- Community Property / Civil Procedure / Evidence / Constitutional Law / Legal Responsibility / Trial Fundamentals (32 units) / FOURTH YEAR- Family Law / Mortgages / Federal Income Taxation / Conflict of Laws / Federal Courts / Debtor & Creditor Law / Administrative Law (32 units) / ELECTIVES- International Law / Labor Law / Immigration Law / Environmental Law / Performance Testing (4 units each)
Comments	REASONABLE Tuition Rates. Adequate catalog materials for initial evaluation, but further contact with school necessary. Incarcerated students. The four-year program necessitates a commitment of approximately 20 hours per week of study. While curriculum fulfills California Bar Exam requirements, it "does not satisfy the requirements of other states for admission to the practice of law" (page 30 of catalog). This is not a "diploma mill."
	*"If licensing is the ultimate goal of the student, the University strongly advises their students to check with their respective state, school district or professional associations for specific requirements" (page 5 of catalog).
	**Newport University School of Law is registered with the Committee of Bar Examiners of the State of California as a correspondence law school. NU advises the "Non-Bar" option as the most viable for incarcerated students.

Stratford Career Institute

P.O. Box 875 Champlain NY 12919-0875
800-363-0058
www.scitraining.com

Program	Legal Assistant / Paralegal
Certification	Yes
Accreditation	"Programs are intended to help individuals in the furtherance of their vocational training and are not intended to be substitutes for state licensing or certification requirements..."
Affiliations	None
Tuition	$849.00 (Tuition Payment plan) avaliable
Text Costs	All materials included
Time Limits	Not Listed
Transfer Hours	No
Curriculum	"The student begins with an exploration of US law, then learns the details of how a law office is organized and operates on a day-to-day basis, with emphasis on the role of the legal assistant within the office."
Comments	Impossible to evaluate tuition rate. Scanty catalog materials. Questionable if this diploma would meet state agency requirements, but program may provide sufficient training to work in a law office.

The Paralegal Institute

18275 North 59th Ave, Ste. 186, Glendale AZ 85308
800-354-1254 / 602-212-0501
www.theparalegalinstitute.com

Program	Criminal Justice Diploma Program (1,350 Clock Hours)
Certification	Yes: Diploma (30 hours)*
Accreditation	Distance Education & Training Council
Affiliations	National Association of Legal Assistants
Tuition	$2,850.00 (Payment plan available) (ER: $95.00) / $97.00 enrollment application fee
Text Costs	Course materials included + S&H fees included as well (makes effective tuition rate even better!)
Time Limits	Maximum 12 months / One 6 month extension
Transfer Hours	NO only applicable towards Associate Degree
Curriculum	Criminal Justice / Criminal Law/ Crime & Drugs / Criminal Procedures / Laws & Evidence / Ethics / Constitutional Law / Criminal Investigation / Juvenile Delinquency / Prevention of Crime
Description	The Paralegal Institute's career development programs are designed to meet the needs of legal professionals. The program provides an interdisciplinary approach to understanding a complex and pluralistic society by explaining the concepts of social control and resolutions available in criminal justice, including current procedures and future changes.
Comments	EXCELLENT tuition rates. Incarcerated students. Good catalog. Multiple diploma programs that also directly apply (1/2 of required hours) toward Associate Degree programs.
	*American Council on Education accredited hours.

The Paralegal Institute

18275 North 59th Ave, Ste. 186, Glendale AZ 85308
800-354-1254 / 602-212-0501
www.theparalegalinstitute.com

Program	Legal Nurse Consultant Program (1,710 Clock Hours)
Certification	Yes: Diploma (38 hours)*
Accreditation	Distance Education & Training Council
Affiliations	National Association of Legal Assistants
Tuition	$3,610.00 (Payment plan available) (ER: $95.00) $97.00 enrollment application fee
Text Costs	Course materials included + S&H fees included as well (makes effective tuition rate even better!)
Time Limits	Maximum 12-months / One 6-month extension
Transfer Hours	NO: only applicable towards Associate Degree
Curriculum	Legal Nurse Consulting: Principles & Practices (25 credit hours) / Legal Research (3) / Legal Analysis & Writing (3) / Litigation & Trial Practice (3) / Torts: Personal Injury Litigation
Description	The program provides a foundation in legal studies and examines the roles of Legal Nurse Consultants in a variety of practice environments. Graduates can practice independently, work in a law firm, as a case manager for an insurance company or a health maintenance organization, or hospitals and clinics as the primary investigators of potential and filed claims involving medical malpractice, personal injury, toxic tort and product liability.
Comments	EXCELLENT tuition rates. Incarcerated students. Good catalog. Multiple diploma programs that also directly apply (1/2 of required hours) toward Associate Degree programs. Possible alternative for those who have had prerequisite credentials, but are now unable to utilize them directly due to felony conviction.

*American Council on Education accredited hours./ **Candidates for admission must present a copy of their credentials (R.N., B.S.N., or M.D.)

The Paralegal Institute

18275 North 59th Ave, Ste. 186, Glendale AZ 85308
800-354-1254 / 602-212-0501
www.theparalegalinstitute.com

Program	Paralegal Studies Program (2,750 Clock Hours)
Certification	Yes: Associate Degree (60 hours)*
Accreditation	Distance Education & Training Council
Affiliations	National Association of Legal Assistants
Tuition	$5,700 (Payment plan available) (ER: $95.00) $97.00 enrollment application fee
Text Costs	Course materials included + S&H fees included as well (makes effective tuition rate even better!)
Time Limits	Maximum 24 months/ One 6-month extension
Transfer Hours	YES Maximum 15 credit hours
Curriculum	Paralegal Today / Legal Research/ Legal Analysis & Writing / Litigation & Trial Practice / Business Organizations / Domestic Relations / Criminal Law / Real Property / Trusts, Wills & Estate Administration / Contracts / Torts: Personal Injury Litigation/ Bankruptcy / Social Security Disability / Administrative Law / Environmental Law/ English / Technical Communications / Business Management/ Mathematics Essentials / Psychology
Description	Program provides a foundation in legal studies that builds upon the Paralegal Diploma Program, and offers a competitive edge in graduate's employability. Completion of the program qualifies graduate to sit for the Certified Legal Assistant Exam administered by the National Association of Legal Assistants.
Comments	EXCELLENT tuition rates. Incarcerated students. Good catalog. Multiple diploma programs that also directly apply (1/2 of required hours) toward Associate Degree programs.

*American Council on Education accredited hours.

The Paralegal Institute

18275 North 59th Ave, Ste. 186, Glendale AZ 85308
800-354-1254 / 602-212-0501
www.theparalegalinstitute.com

Program	Paralegal Diploma Program (1350 Clock Hours)
Certification	Yes: Diploma (30 hours)*
Accreditation	Distance Education & Training Council
Affiliations	National Association of Legal Assistants
Tuition	$2,850.00 (Payment plan available) (ER: $95.00) / $97.00 enrollment application fee
Text Costs	Course materials included + S&H fees included as well (makes effective tuition rate even better!)
Time Limits	Maximum 12-months/ One 6-month extension
Transfer Hours	NO: only applicable towards Associates Degree
Curriculum	Paralegal Today / Legal Research / Legal Analysis & Writing / Litigation & Trial Practice / Business Organizations / Domestic Relations / Criminal Law / Real Property / Trusts, Wills & Estate Administration/ Contracts
Description	Program provides a foundation in legal studies. Completion of the program qualifies graduate to sit for the Certified Legal Assistant Exam administered by the National Association of Legal Assistants.
Comments	EXCELLENT tuition rates. Incarcerated students. Good catalog. Multiple diploma programs that also directly apply (1/2 of required hours) toward Associate Degree programs.

*American Council on Education accredited hours.

University of Wisconsin
Independent Study

505 South Rosa Road Suite 200, Madison WI 53719-1277
877-895-3276 / 608-262-2011
www.wisc.edu

Founded	1892 (one of the nation's original distance education programs)
Program	Distance Education Program
Certification	Yes: Certificate of Completion
Accreditation	North Central Association of Colleges & Schools
Affiliations	None noted
Tuition	$150.00 per course + $55 admin fee (ER: $14.65)
Text Costs	Bibliography listed (Author/ text/ publication date)
Time Limits	Maximum 12 months / 3 months @ $25.00 / 2nd @ $50.00
Transfer Hours	Non-Applicable
Curriculum	A305 Legal & Regulatory Environment (14 CEUs) / A306 Business Law (14 CEUs)
Description	A305 Topics covered deal mostly with public governmental regulation of business, but also include areas of private law such as agency, partnerships, and corporations with a close connection to publically regulated areas. This course assumes no previous experience with business law. A306 Course covers areas of business law involved in private business relationships. Course is recommended for those preparing for accountancy and the CPA examination. NOTE: This course does not cover three areas important to preparation for the CPA exam: agency, partnerships and corporations. Those areas are covered in A305.
Comments	EXCELLENT tuition rates. Good catalog. Well-designed courses.

Undergraduate Programs (Colleges & Universities)

Acadia University
Continuing & Distance Education

38 Crowell Drive Wolfville, Nova Scotia B4P 2R6
800-565-6568 / 902-585-1434
conted.acadiau.ca

Founded	1838 (Catalog 2007-2008)
Accreditation	Unknown
External Degree	None
Tuition	Not Listed (ER: Unknown)
Text Costs	Not listed / No bibliography in catalog
Time Limits	Not Listed
Transfer Hours	Non-Applicable
Curriculum	Business (2 courses) Computers (3) Education (5) Geology (1) History (3) Independant Study (1) Nutrition (1) Political Sciences (1) Psychology (3) Sociology (6)
Comments	Inadequate brochure/catalog. Not nearly enough information to offer much of an analysis. Prime example of school shifting to online programming that hasn't yet totally given up on correspondence study, but nearly there.

Adams State College
Extended Studies

208 Edgemont Boulevard Alamosa CO 81102
800-548-6679 / 719-587-7671
www.adams.edu

Founded	Unknown (Catalog: 2007-2008)
Accreditation	North Central Association of Colleges & Schools
External Degree	Associate of Arts / Associate of Science (60 credits) Bachelor of Arts in: Business Administration / Interdisciplinary Studies / Sociology (120) Bachelor of Science in Business Administration (120 credits)
Tuition	$120.00 per credit hour (ER: $120.00) $25.00 degree program application fee
Text Costs	Not Listed
Time Limits	Maximum 1 year / Minimum 6 weeks
Transfer Hours	45 credits per AA / 90 credits per BA/S / "Free Unofficial Evaluation" of accumulated transfer credits / CLEP / Military Experience / Non-Accredited Credits Policy
Curriculum	Art (1 course) Business (27) Criminal Justice (9) English (19) Economics (3) Environmental Science (1) Exercise Physiology, Leisure Science (1) Geology (1) Government (4) History, Government, Philosophy (2) History (8) Interdivisional (2) Math (7) Philosophy (1) Psychology (1) Sociology (28)
Comments	VERY GOOD tuition rates. Good catalog. Incarcerated students. Extensive offerings in: Business, Criminal Justice, English & Sociology. Many certificate programs (see Adams State in other sections).

Andrews University
Enrollment Office

P.O. Box 4437, Silver Spring MD 20914-4437
800-782-4769

Founded	1997 (Catalog: 2007)
Accreditation	North Central Association of Colleges & Schools
External Degree	Associate of Arts General Studies Personal Ministries (62 credits) Bachelor of Arts Humanities / Religion (124 credits) Bachelor of Science Cross-Cultural Studies (124 credits) Human Organization and Behavior
Tuition	$280.00 per credit / $70.00 per enrollment fee (ER: $303.33) Senior Citizens (60+) 50% tuition discount program
Text Costs	Listed with full bibliography & order form / Used Book Discount Policy (usually 30% off new retail)
Time Limits	Maximum 1 year / 1 year extension @ $50.00
Transfer Hours	AA 45 hours / BA/S 90 hours / ACE / CLEP / Experiential Learning
Curriculum	Behavioral Sciences (14 courses) Communications (1) English (6) Geography (1) History & Political Science (8) Interdisciplinary Studies (2) International Language Studies (3) Mathematics (3) Music (1) Nutrition (1) Physics (1) Religion & Biblical Studies (20)
Comments	HIGH tuition rates. Good catalog. Graduation & Departmental Honors program. Book buy-back program: 30%-50% of current retail price.

Ashworth College

430 Technology Parkway Norcross GA 30092
800-6409524
www.ashworthcollege.edu

Founded	1987 (Catalog 2007-2008)
Accreditation	Distance Education & Training Council
External Degree	Associate Degree in Accounting / Business Management (60 credits) / Computer Information Management / Construction Management / Criminal Justice / Early Childhood Education / Finance / Health Care Management / Human Resource Management / Marketing / Psychology / Security Management
Tuition	$1200 for degree program (ER: $20)
Text Costs	Included in tuition price
Time Limits	Minimum 6 months / Maximum 4 years / Extensions for fee
Transfer Hours	45 credits / CLEP / DANTES / ACE
Curriculum	Classes limited to specific degree program. Must be enrolled in degree program to take courses from this school.
Comments	OUTSTANDING tuition rates, with this caveat: Uncertain how many of these credits will be transferable and/or degree programs accepted by other schools. Good gerenal catalog, with specific materials for each degree program. School claims more than 750,000 graduates worldwide.

Brigham Young University Independent Study

120 Morris Center, Provo UT 84602-1514
800-914-8931 / 801-422-2868
www.byu.edu

Founded	1978 (Catalog: 2007 – 2008)
Accreditation	Northwest Association of Colleges & Schools
External Degree	None
Tuition	$137.00 (ER: $137.00)
Text Costs	Listed / Full bibliography including ISBN#s
Time Limits	Maximum 1 year / 3-month extension @$20.00 fee
Transfer Hours	Non-Applicable
Curriculum	Accounting (4 courses) American Heritage (1) Anthropology (4) Art History & Curatorial Studies (2) Biology (4) Business Management (4) Chemical Engineering (1) Chemistry (1) Civil & Environmental Engineering (3) Communication Disorders (1) Communications (6) Construction Management (1) Dance (2) Economics (1) Education: Counseling, Psychology & Special Education (10) Educational Leadership & Foundations (1) Elementary Education (8) Instructional Psychology & Technology (2) Secondary Education (4) English (27) Exercise Science (6) French (1) Geography (4) Geological Sciences (2) German (2) Health (2) Health & Physical Education (1) History (21) Home & Family Living (1) Humanities (3) Languages (4) Management Communications (1) Managerial Economics (2) Marriage, Family & Human Development (3) Mathematics (6) Microbiology & Molecular Biology (1) Music (10) Near Eastern Studies (1) Nursing (1) Nutrition, Dietetics & Food Science (1) Organizational Behavior (4) Philosophy (3) Physical Science (1) Physics & Astronomy (5) Physiology & Developmental Biology (1) Plant & Animal Wildlife Sciences (3) Political Science (7) Psychology (17) Religious Education: Ancient Scripture (6) Church History & Doctrine (10) Social Work (1) Sociology (1) Spanish (1) Statistics (1) Student Development (4) Theater & Media Arts (3) Visual Arts-Studio (1)
Comments	VERY GOOD tuition rates. Well done catalog. BYU Bookstore buy-back program, 50% of retail price. Extensive offerings in: Education, English, History, Music, Psychology & (naturally) Religious Education. School has top notch academic reputation. Many personal enrichment courses; refer to BYU in Vocational Section.

California Coast University

700 North Mail Street, Santa Ana CA 92701
888-228-8648 / 714-547-9625
www.calcoast.edu

Founded	1973
Accreditation	Distance Education & Training Council
External Degree	Associate of Science – Business Administration / Psychology (60 credits)
	Bachelor of Science – Business Administration / Management / Health Care Administration / Psychology (126 credits)
Tuition	$110.00 per credit hour [Continental U.S.] (ER: $110.00) $130.00 per credit hour [Outside Continental U.S.] (ER: $130.00) (Tuition Payment Plan available)
Text Costs	Not Listed / No Bibliography / Textbook rental program!
Time Limits	Minimum 9 months for degree / Maximum 5 years for degree
Transfer Hours	30 credits for A.S. / 93 credits for B.S. Experiential Credit (30 credits) CLEP / DANTES / ACE / TECEP
Curriculum	Business Administration (16 courses) Health Care Administration (6 courses) Psychology (4 courses)
Comments	VERY GOOD tuition rates. Catalog explains programs well. This school is structured to service the more life-experienced and self-starting student. All degree-seeking students will have to transfer previous earned or verifiable credits. CCU courses encompass a study guide with recommended texts and a self-study outline. Timed exams are proctored with "students permitted to utilize any notes, study guides, calculators, or other material used during the completion of their course work" (p.6). NOTE: From experience this is not as easy as it seems.
Special Features	"Credits and degrees earned through CCU are recognized for promotions, assignments, and position qualification standards, within the US military and Federal government" (p.3 catalog).

Catholic Distance University

120 East Colonial Highway, Hamilton VA 20158
888-254-4CDU / 540-338-2700
www.cdu.edu

Founded	1983 (2007-2008)
Accreditation	Distance Education & Training Council / NCEA
External Degree	Catechetical Diploma (36 credits) Bachelor of Arts in Theology (126 credits)
Tuition	$227.00 per credit hour (ER: $227.00) $150.00 annual technology fee; will increase "ER" rate
Text Costs	Average $25.00 / Course Bibliography listed. Catechism of the Catholic Church & Catholic Bible required for all courses
Time Limits	3 to 6 months / Extension @ full tuition fee / 6 years to complete certificate & degree programs
Transfer Hours	90 credits for BA program
Curriculum	Church & Theology (18 courses)
Comments	AVERAGE tuition rates. Good text prices. Good catalog. Incarcerated students. Highly focused degree program. Opportunity to qualify for Delta Epsilon Tau: Inernational Honor Society for Distance Learning.
	NOTE: course materials shipped in 3-ring binders thus you may need to make special arrangements due to your facility's property restrictions.

Charter Oak State College
Degrees Without Boundaries

55 Paul J. Manafort Drive, New Britian CT 06053-2150
860-832-3855
www.charteroak.edu

Founded	1973 (2007-2008)
Accreditation	New England Association of Colleges and Schools
External Degree	Associate in Science / Arts (60-credits) Bachelor of Science / Arts (120 credits)
Tuition	Irrelevant (all online courses) Fees for "credit banking / degree" ????
Text Costs	Non-Applicable
Time Limits	Non-Applicable
Transfer Hours	Unlimited! CLEP / DANTES / ACE / PONSI Not required to take courses to fulfill degree.
Curriculum	All online
Comments	Unable to evaluate fee structure. This program has changed dramatically since the previous edition. School is still a credit bank, but with nearly all services online it is hard to know how a prisoner-student with exceptional credit hours could utilize its services to coalesce a degre. It's a shame, since this was once a real viable option for the life-experience prisoner-student to earn a degree.

Cleveland Institute of Electronics

1776 East 17th Street, Cleveland OH 44114-3679
800-243-6446 / 216-781-9400
www.cic-wc.edu

Founded	1934 (as Practical Radio Institute) (Catalog 2007)
Accreditation	Distance Education & Training Council / AC / CHEA
External Degree	Associate in Applied Science in Computer Information Technology & Systems Management (96 credits)
Tuition	$3,540.00 for degree program (ER: $36.87) (Financing plan option @ 14% with 35 $125 payments) (Self-paced & if you complete all lessons in 1 term it's all you pay for your degree! Good option especially if you have applicable transferable credit hours to shorten required curriculum.)
Text Costs	Included with tuition! Makes it an even better deal!
Time Limits	Maximum Eight 24 week term / Extensions with nominal fee
Transfer Hours	Maximum 72 credit hours
Curriculum	206 Lesson: Introduction to Computer / Operating System / Fundamentals of Information System / Introduction to the Internet & World Wide We / Computer Hardware (A+ Certification / Computer Networking (Network + Certification / PIC Controlle / Algebra & Trig / Algebra & Trig I / Technical Physic / Technical Writing / Technical Writing I / Principles of Micro-economic / General Psycholog / Introduction to Managemen / Data Communication / Computer Applications in Busines / Information & Technology – The Network Econom / Management Information Systems*
Comments	VERY GOOD tuition rates. Very good catalog materials. Don't know how it is arranged (depending on specific institution's restrictions), but school has many incarcerated students. Solid looking technical degree program. Must work through all clearances at your particular institution before enrollment. Send requests specifically to: Andrew S. Podsiadlo Jr, Guidance Counselor. Students graduating with grade averages 90%+ are eligible for membership in Alpha Beta Kappa Society. The Institute of Electrical & Electronics Engineers (IEES) also offers membership to students.

*Individual courses not available; must enroll in degree program. (See: CIE in Vocational section for particular programs.)

Cleveland Institute of Electronics

1776 East 17th Street, Cleveland OH 44114-3679
800-243-644 / 216-781-9400
www.cic-wc.edu

Founded	1934 (as Practical Radio Institute) (Catalog 2007)
Accreditation	Distance Education & Training Counci / AC / CHEA
External Degree	Associate in Applied Science in Electronic Engineering Technology (106 credits)
Tuition	$3,540.00 for degree program (ER: $36.87) (Financing plan option @ 14% with 35 $125 payments) (Self-paced & if you complete all lessons in 1 term it's all you pay for your degree! Good option especially if you have applicable transferable credit hours to shorten required curriculum.)
Text Costs	Included with tuition! Makes it an even better deal!
Time Limits	Maximum Eight 24 week term / Extensions with nominal fee
Transfer Hours	Maximum 80 credit hours
Curriculum	254 Lessons: Current & Voltag / Static Electricit / Tracing Wiring on Printed Circuit Board / Relays & Robot / Transformer / Rectifiers & Amplifier / Phasers & Formula / Resonance Filter / Oscillator / Digital Switching Unit / Pulse Processing Unit / Pulse Processing Circuit / Sequential Logic Circuit / Color Symptom Troubleshootin / Fundamentals of Boolean Algebra / ROMs & PROMs & PLA / Network Theorem / Field Effect Transistors, etc.
Comments	VERY GOOD tuition rates. Very good catalog materials. Don't know how it is arranged (depending on specific institution's restrictions), but school has many incarcerated students. Solid looking technical degree program. Must work through all clearances at your particular institution before enrollment. Send requests specifically to: Andrew S. Podsiadlo Jr, Guidance Counselor. Students graduating with grade averages 90%+ are eligible for membership in Alpha Beta Kappa Society. The Institute of Electrical & Electronics Engineers (IEES) also offers membership to students. ***Must have access to an oscilloscope to complete degree program.
	*Individual courses not available; must enroll in degree program. (see: CIE in Vocational section for particular programs)

Colorado State University
Pueblo Continuing Education Division

2200 Bonforte Blvd Pueblo, CO 81001
800-388-6154 / 719-549-2316
www.colostate-pueblo.edu

Founded	Unknown (Catalog: 2007-2008)
Accreditation	North Central Association of Colleges & Schools
External Degree	Bachelor of Science in Sociology (120 credits) / Bachelor of Science in Social Sciences (120 credits) / Bachelor of Science in Sociology / Criminology (120 credits)
Tuition	$139.00 per hour (ER: $139.00)
Text Costs	Not Listed/ No bibliography / $75 video tape for some courses
Time Limits	Minimum 12-weeks / Maximum 6 months / 6-month extension @ $40.00
Transfer Hours	Yes: Up to 90 credits / ACE / CLEP / DANTES / Credit by Examination; "Unofficial" credit evaluation service
Curriculum	Anthropology (2 courses) Art (1) Biology (4) Business (1) Chemistry (3) Economics (2) Education (7) English / Speech (10) Geography (3) Geology (2) History (4) Mathematics (1) Management (10) Marketing (4) Nursing (3) Political Science (8) Psychology (6) Social Science (1) Sociology (28)
Comments	VERY GOOD tuition rates. Adequate catalog. Incarcerated students. Extensive offerings in English/Speech, Management & Sociology. "Unofficial" transfer credit evaluation service may be worth the preparation effort just for the unbiased review of what you can compile.

Colorado State University
Division of Continuing Education

Spruce Hall 1040 Campus Delivery, Fort Collins CO 80523-1040
877-491-4336 / 970-491-5288
www.learn.colostate.edu

Founded	1967
Accreditation	North Central Association of Colleges & Schools
External Degree	None via correspondence / all online
Tuition	Not listed – varies
Text Costs	Not listed
Time Limits	Maximum 6 months / 6-month extension
Transfer Hours	Non-Applicable
Curriculum	Agriculture (2 courses) Construction Management (1) Design & Merchandising (1) Economics (1) Education (1) Fishery & Wildlife & Biology (3) Human Development & Family Studies (2) History (1) Mechanical Engineering (1) Psychology (3) Soil & Crop Sciences (3)
Comments	UNKNOWN tuition rates. Incarcerated students. Another school that has nearly phased out correspondence study. Catalog can be confusing and lacking relevant information. Prisoners may be eligible for "John C. Snider" and "Colorado Commission on Higher Education Extended Studies" scholarships. Contact school for requirements.

Columbia Union College
Enrollment Office
c/o Griggs University

P.O. Box 4437, Silver Spring MD 20914-4437
800-782-4769 / 301-680-6590

Founded	1969 (Catalog 2007)
Accreditation	Middlestone Association of Colleges & Schools
External Degree	Associate of Arts: Minor-Business Administration (60 credits) Associate of Science: Minor-Psychology (60 credits) Bachelor of Arts: General Studies (120 credits) Psychology / Religion / Theology / Bachelor of Science: Business Administration / General Studies (120 credits) $50.00 degree program application fee
Tuition	$280.00 per credit / $70.00 enrollment fee (ER: $303.33) Senior citizens (60+) 50% tuition discount program
Text Costs	Listed with full bibliography & order form / Used Book Discount Policy (usually 30% off new retail)
Time Limits	Maximum 1 year / 1-year extension @ $50.00
Transfer Hours	AA 45 hours / BA/S 90 hours / ACE / CLEP / Experiential Learning
Curriculum	Accounting (2 courses) Biology (3) Business (4) Communication (2) Computer Science (1) Economics (2) Education (2) English (5) Finance (1) Foods/Nutrition (1) French (4) Geography (1) Health Science (2) History (6) Management (4) Marketing (1) Mathematics (5) Music (1) Physics (1) Political Science (1) Psychology (14) Religion (27)
Comments	HIGH tuition rates. Good catalog. Graduation & Departmental Honors program. Book buy-back program, 30%-50% of current retail price.

Global University

1211 Glenstone Avenue, Springfield MO 65804
800-443-1083 / 417-862-9533
www.globaluniversity.edu

Founded	1967 (Catalog Info: 2007)
Accreditation	Distance Education Training Council / Council for Higher Education Accreditation
External Degree	Certificates: Bible Interpreter, Christian Communicator, Christian Mission (17 credits), Certificate in Bible Theology (32 credits), Diploma in Ministry (64 credits), Diploma in Theology (96 credits) Associate of Arts* – Religious Studies, Bible/Theology (64 credits), Associate* – Church Ministries, Ministerial Studies (66 credits), Bachelor of Arts – Bible & Theology, Religious Missions, Bible/Pastoral Ministries & Honors degrees (128 credits), 2nd Bachelor of Arts – in all fields (50 credits), (except Bible/Pastoral Ministries) Honors degrees (70 credits)
Tuition	$99.00 per credit / 20% PRISONER DISCOUNT / $10 course fee (ER: $82.53) $40.00 Program Application Fee / Graduation Application Fee $25.00
Text Costs	Listed / Study Guides $33.94 / Text Avgs $50.00 per course
Time Limits	Maximum 6 months / 6-month extension $50.00 fee
Transfer Hours	32 credits for AAs & 96 credits for BAs
Curriculum	Bible (30) Theology (15) Church Ministries (22) Missions (8) Business (1) Communications (3) Education (2) English (3) Geological Sciences (2) History (7) Health Science (2) Leadership (3) Literature (3) Mathematics (2) Music (1) Philosophy (1) Religion (2) Sociology (2)
Comments	EXCELLENT tuition rates! Good catalog & materials. Incarcerated students & assigned representative (one of the few schools to have such). If bible/theological study is your forte, this is a great school. * Meets USA ministerial license requirements

Governors State University
School of Extended Learning

1 University Parkway, University Park IL 60466-0975
708-534-1099
www.govst.edu/sxl

Founded	Unknown (2007 – 2008)
Accreditation	North Central Association of Colleges and Schools
External Degree	None
Tuition	$153.00 per credit + $26.00 per credit fees (ER: $174.00) $28.00 per trimester computer technology fee for all students
Text Costs	Not listed / No Bibliography
Time Limits	Non- Applicable
Transfer Hours	Unknown
Curriculum	English (3 courses) International Culture (2)
Comments	GOOD tuition rates. Poor catalog. Another example of shift to near-total reliance on online access/service.

Graduate School USDA
Self-Paced Training

P.O. Box 25605, Denver CO 80225-0605
888-744-GRAD
www.grad.usda.gov.

Founded	1921 (Catalog: 2007-2008)
Accreditation	American Council on Education / College Credit Recommendation Service
External Degree	Certificate of Accomplishment in: Basic Accounting (14 credits) Advanced Accounting (26 credits) Federal Government Accounting (14 credits) Meteorology (33/45 credits)
Tuition	$118.33 / $147.50 per credit hour (ER: $118.33 / $147.50)
Text Costs	Not Listed
Time Limits	Maximum 1 year / 1-year extension @ $50.00
Transfer Hours	One third of required credits
Curriculum	Accounting (14 courses) Editing (3) Engineering & Technology (3) Library & Indexing Techniques (7) Mathematics (6) Meteorology (7) Paralegal Studies (7)
Comments	VERY GOOD tuition rates. Good catalog. Incarcerated students. Well-developed correspondence program. Extensive personal development CEU credit programs as well (see vocational section)

Huntington College of Health Sciences

1204-D Kenesaw, Knoxville TN 37919
800 290-4226 / 865 524-8079
www.hchs.edu

Founded	1985 (Catalog 2007)
Accreditation	Distance Education & Training Council / ACE
External Degree	Diploma in Comprehensive Nutrition (18 credits) / Diploma in Sports Nutrition (18 credits) / Diploma in Women's Nutrition (18 credits) / Diploma in Small Business Management (18 credits) / Diploma in Natural Sciences (18 credits) Associate of Science in Applied Nutrition (60 credits) / Bachelor of Health Science in Nutrition (127 credits)
Tuition	$2970.00 per Diploma program (ER: $165.00) / $9900.00 for Associate Degree program (ER: $165.00) / $20,955.00 for Bachelor Degree Program (ER: $165.00) (Tuition payment plan available)
Text Costs	Diploma in Comprehensive Nutritional Program ($550.00) / Diploma in Women's Nutritional Program ($500.00) / Diploma in Small Business Management Program ($375.00) / Diploma in Natural Sciences Program ($425.00) Associate of Science in Applied Nutrition ($10350.00) / Bachelor of Health Science Degree in Nutrition ($4945.00) (Estimated cost of textbooks, materials, S&H per program)
Time Limits	Maximum 4 months per course / 3-month extension @ $50.00 / Diploma Program 15 months / Associate Degree 48 months
Transfer Hours	Diploma Programs 6 credits / Associate Degree 30 credits / Bachelor Degree 95 credits / ACE / ACT PEP / CLEP
Curriculum	Biological Sciences (5 courses) Business Administration (2) Chemistry (2) Child Development (1) Communications (1) English (3) Exercise Science (1) Health Sciences (8) Herbal Sciences (3) Mathematics (4) Nutritional Sciences (3) Nutritional Science (19) Psychology (1) Social Sciences (1)
Comments	GOOD tuition rates. Good catalog though 10 course text bibliographies are available via website; you'll need to write. Incarcerated students. Extensive offerings in: Nutritional Science. Many well-paying Health Care industry positions such as these programs are available to ex-felons. If this field is of interest, check out this school.

Indiana University
School of Continuing Studies

Owen Hall 001 790 East Kirkwood Avenue, Bloomington IN 47405-7101
800-334-1011 / 812-855-2292
www.indiana.edu

Founded	1975 (Catalog: 2007-2008)
Accreditation	North Central Association of Colleges & Schools
External Degree	Health Care Accounting & Financial Management Certificate (9 hours) Associate of Arts in General Studies (60 hours) Bachelor of General Studies (120 credits)
Tuition	$145.00 Resident credit hour / $65.00 fee per course (ER: $166.72) $164.22 nonresident credit hour / $65.00 course fee (ER: $185.88) / $50.00 degree application fee
Text Costs	Not listed / Course learning guides $25.00
Time Limits	Maximum 1 year / Two 6-month extensions
Transfer Hours	45 hours applied to Associate Degree / 90 hours applied to Bachelor Degree / "Self-Acquired Competency" (SAC) credit (i.e. Life Experience) / AP / CLEP / DANTES / ACT-PEP Regents / Credit by Examination.
Curriculum	Accounting (3 courses) Arts & Sciences Career Services (1) Astronomy (3) Biology (2) Business (12) Classical Studies (5) Communication & Culture (3) Comparative Literature (2) Computer Science (1) Criminal Justice (5) Economics (3) Education (4) English (27) Fine Arts (2) Folklore & Ethnomusicology (3) French (2) Gender Studies (1) Geography (6) Geological Sciences (4) Health, Physical Education & Recreation (6) History (23) History & Philosophy of Science (1) Journalism (2) Linguistics (1) Mathematics (9) Music (3) Near Eastern Languages & Culture (1) Nursing (1) Philosophy (7) Physics (3) Political Science (8) Psychological & Brain Sciences (6) Religious Studies (5) Sociology (9) Spanish (4)
Comments	GOOD tuition rates. Good catalog. Incarcerated students. Extensive offerings in: Accounting, Business, English, History, Mathematics, Philosophy, Sociology. One of the most comprehensive correspondence courses in the nation. Degrees award with earned "Distinction" honor, Dean's list recognition program. Internationally respected university; good program to transfer less-expensive maximum allowable hours to then earn degree from.

Lee University
Center for Adult & Professional Studies

100 Eighth Street NE, Cleveland TN 37311-2235
800-256-5916 / 423-614-8370
www.leeuniversity.edu

Founded	1976 (Catalog: 2007-2008)
Accreditation	North Central Association of Colleges & Schools
External Degree	None
Tuition	$276.00 / $15.00 registration & $20 extension fee (ER: $288.00)
Text Costs	Not Listed
Time Limits	Maximum 4 months / 4-month extension @ $20.00
Transfer Hours	Non-Applicable
Curriculum	Art (1 course) Bible (16) Biology (1) Christian Education (10) Christian Leadership (12) Church History (3) English (3) Greek (2) History (3) Humanities (7) Intercultural Studies (2) Mathematics (1) Music (1) Pastoral Ministry (12) Physical Science (1) Psychology (1) Sociology (1) Speech (1) Theology (12)
Comments	HIGH tuition rates. Poor catalog materials. Extensive offerings in: Bible, Christian Education, Christian Leadership, Pastoral Ministry & Theology.

Life Pacific College
Distance Learning Department

1100 West Covina Blvd, San Dimas CA 91773
877-851-0900 / 909-706-3059
www.lifepacific.edu

Founded	1924 – by "Aimee Semple McPherson" (Catalog: 2006-2007)
Accreditation	Western Association of Schools & Colleges
External Degree	Christian Worker Certificate (13 credits) Christian Ministry Certificate (32 credits) Associate of Arts Degree (64 credits)
Tuition	$120.00 per credit & includes all fees (ER: 120.00)
Text Costs	Included with costs
Time Limits	6 months / 6-month extension @ $25.00 fee
Transfer Hours	32 credits / $35.00 degree program application fee
Curriculum	Bible (8 courses) Theology (4 courses) Ministry (4 courses) General Education (5 courses)
Comments	VERY GOOD tuition rates, particularly with materials included! Good catalog. Focused program & school. LPC "offers a Scholarship Program to students. ... [and] can receive a scholarship for up to 64 units of independent study courses. ... Contact the Distance Learning Center for more details."
Special Features	LPC offers the "Group Study Institute" (GSI) which is designed to enable the local church (or possibly prison chapel?) to offer college-level courses for credit to their congregation. Individuals will benefit from the challenge of college-level course work within a classroom setting of mutually committed friends. The organization is able to offer a pre-designed and regulated program through Pacific Life College.

Louisiana State University
Independent & Distance Learning

1225 Pleasant Hall, Baton Rouge LA 70803
800-234-5046 / 225-578-3171
www.lsu.edu

Founded	1924 (Catalog Info: Spring 2007)
Accreditation	Southern Association of Colleges & Schools
External Degree	Certificate of Program Completion (15 hours) (undergraduate) Business Communication / Human Services / Liberal Studies
Tuition	$73.00 per credit hour / $10.00 per course fee (ER: $76.33)
Text Costs	Not listed / Referrals to 5 book stores
Time Limits	Maximum nine months / One 3-month extension ($25.00 fee)
Transfer Hours	Non-Applicable
Curriculum	Accounting (10) African-American Studies (1) Anthropology (2) Biological Sciences (3) Business Law (2) Classical Studies (1) Communication Studies (2) Curriculum & Instruction (1) Dairy Science (1) Economics (5) Educational Leadership, Research & Counseling (1) English (17) Environmental Management Systems (1) Environmental Studies (1) Finance (2) French (4) Geography (2) Geology (2) German (5) History (9) Human Resource Education (8) Information Systems & Decision Sciences (1) Kinesiology (3) Latin (2) Library & Information Sciences (1) Management (5) Marketing (8) Mass Communication (1) Mathematics (15) Military Science (1) Music (1) Philosophy (2) Physical Science (2) Physics (2) Political Science (5) Psychology (8) Religious Studies (1) Sociology (5) Spanish (5) Theater (1) COLLEGE PREPARATORY NONCREDIT COURSES: English (2) Mathematics (7) Social Work (1) Study Skills (1)
Comments	EXCELLENT tuition rates! Extensive distance education experience (13,000 annual enrollments). Incarcerated students currently enrolled (including me!), registered testing site at Angola State Penitentiary. Course Fact Sheets (i.e. curriculum & text bibliography) available upon request. Extensive offerings in Accounting, English, History, Management/Marketing, Mathematics. Good catalog & good student services.

Moody Bible Institution
Moody Distance Learning Center
820 North LaSalle Blvd, Chicago IL 60610
800-758-6352 / 312-329-4262

Founded	1909 (Catalog: 2007-2008)
Accreditation	Higher Education Commission of the North Central Association / Association for Biblical Higher Education
External Degree	Certificate of Biblical Studies (30 credits) Associate of Biblical Studies (60 credits) Bachelor of Science in Biblical Studies (120 credits)
Tuition	$159.00 per credit hour ($159.00)
Text Costs	Not listed / No course bibliography
Time Limits	6 months / Extensions unknown
Transfer Hours	Up to 75% per certificate/degree
Curriculum	Biblical information (19 courses) Education (3 courses) Evangelism (2 courses) Missions (1 course) Christian Worship (1 course) Personal Communications (1 course) Theology (8 courses)
Comments	GOOD tuition rates. Minimally informative catalog. Comprehensive Biblical study degree program.

Mountain State University

P.O. Box 9003, Beckley WV 25802-9003
800-766-6067 / 304-253-7351
www.mountainstate.edu

Founded	Unknown (2007)
Accreditation	Unknown
External Degree	None
Tuition	$205.00 per credit + $65.00 per credit hour fee (ER: $270.00)
Text Costs	Not listed / No bibliography
Time Limits	Unknown
Transfer Hours	Not Applicable
Curriculum	Accounting (11 courses) Art (5) Astronomy (1) Aviation (8) Banking (1) Biology (26) Business Law (4) Chemistry (12) Computer Information Systems (2) Communications (7) Criminal Justice (23) Computer Systems and Computer Information (3) Economics (4) Emerging Systems (1) English (15) Environmental Science (14) Finance (5) Forensics (1) Geography (12) Geology (3) Health Care (5) Health Care Management (2) History (15) Health (5) Health Education (5) Humanities (7) Information Technology (20) Legal Systems (8) Medical Administration (13) Mathematics (13) Meteorology (1) Management (15) Marketing (12) Nursing (15) Office Administration (12) Paralegal (2) Philosophy (2) Physical Science (5) Physics (3) Political Science (4) Psychology (17) Religion (5) Respiration (2) Sociology (6) Social Work (4)
Comments	HIGH tuition rates. Poor catalog/materials making it almost impossible to evaluate. Extensive offerings in: Accounting / Biology / Chemistry / Criminal Justice / English / Environmental Science / Geography / History / Information Technology / Medical Administration / Mathematics / Management / Marketing / Nursing / Office Management / Psychology.

Newport University

4101 Westerly Place, Suite #103, Newport Beach CA, 92660
949-757-1155
www.newport.edu

Founded	1976 (2007 – 2008)
Accreditation	Approved by the State of California, Bureau of Private Post-Secondary & Vocational Education
External Degree	Associate in Arts (60 credits) Bachelor of Arts (120 credits) Business Administration / Human Behavior
Tuition	$142.00 per credit (ER: $142.00) $100.00 Application fee
Text Costs	Not listed / No bibliography in catalog
Time Limits	Satisfactory progress requires 2 course completions per year
Transfer Hours	Up to 45 credits AA program / 90 credits BA program / CLEP / DANTES / Life Experience Credits, etc.
Curriculum	AA – required courses (3) Natural Science (6) Social Science (7) Humanities (7) Mathematics (4) BA – Business Administration Core Courses (8) Electives (9) BA – Human Behavior Core Courses (6) Electives (13)
Comments	VERY GOOD tuition rates. So-So catalog materials. Incarcerated students. Because of the structure of this school individual courses cannot be taken; must be enrolled in degree program to take classes. Generally a student would be better off enrolling in a public school for their undergraduate work and possibly consider this university for post-baccalaureate degree matriculation. This is not a "diploma mill." Grants of $300.00 – $500.00 per year possible, determined at time of evaluation.

* "If licensing is the ultimate goal of the student, the university strongly advises their students to check with their respective state, school district or professional associations for specific requirements" (page 5 of catalog).

Northern State University
Office of Extended Studies

Spafford Hall 106, 1200 S. Jay Street, Aberdeen SD 57401
800-678-5330 / 605-626-2568
www.northern.edu

Founded	Unknown (Catalog unknown)
Accreditation	Northwest Association of Colleges & Schools
External Degree	None
Tuition	$203.50
Text Costs	Not Listed
Time Limits	Maximum 350 days / Extension & fees unknown
Transfer Hours	Non-Applicable
Curriculum	Business (8 courses) Education Research (1) Elementary Education (1) Educational Psychology (1) Industrial Education (2) Indian Education (1) Industrial Technology (1) Mathematics (8) Methods Teaching Foreign Languages (1) Sociology (2) Spanish (8)
Comments	AVERAGE tuition rates. Incarcerated students. Extensive offerings in Spanish.

Oakwood College
Enrollment Office
C/O Griggs University

P.O. Box 4437, Silver Spring MD 20914-4437
800-782-4769

Founded	1999 (Catalog: 2007)
Accreditation	Southern Association of Colleges & Schools
External Degree	Bachelor of Arts in Interdisciplinary Studies (128 credits) Second Bachelor's Degree (160 credits)
Tuition	$280.00 per credit / $70.00 per enrollment fee (ER: $303.33) Senior Citizens (60+) 50% tuition discount program
Text Costs	Listed with full bibliography & order form / Used book discount policy (usually 30% off new retail)
Time Limits	Maximum 1 year / 1-year extension @ $50.00
Transfer Hours	AA 45 hours / BA/S 90 hours ACE / CLEP / Experiential Learning
Curriculum	Biology (1 course) Business (11) Communications (1) Computer Science (1) Education (3) English (7) Fine Arts (1) Geography (1) Health & Nutrition (2) History & Political Science (7) Languages: Greek (4) French (2) Spanish (2) / Mathematics (3) Physics (1) Psychology & Sociology (10) Religion & Theology (13)
Comments	HIGH tuition rates. Good catalog. Graduation & Departmental Honors program. Book buy-back program, 30%-50% of current retail price.

Ohio University
Life Long & Distance Learning
College Program for the Incarcerated (CPI)

Haning Hall 222, Ohio University, Athens OH 45701-2979
800-444-2910
www.ohio.edu

Founded	1974-CPI (Catalog 2007)
Accreditation	North Central Association of Colleges and Schools / UCEA
External Degree	Associate in Individual Studies (96.5 hours) Associate in Applied Business (96.25 hours) Bachelor of Specialized Studies (192.25 hours)
Tuition	$1125.00 6-8 one quarter credit hours (ER:187.50*) $25.00 application fee which is applied to 1st enrollment / $69.00 per hour Credit by Examination fee (ER: $92.00)
Text Costs	Included with comprehensive fee packages
Time Limits	Maximum 8 months / 4-month extension FREE / 2nd 4-month extension @ $50.00 / No extension required if all lessons completed without final
Transfer Hours	Yes: Up to 66.25 hours for Associate Degree / 148.25 hours for BSS
Curriculum	Accounting (1) Accounting Technology (3) African-American Studies (2) Aviation (5) Biological Sciences (4) Business Law (5) Business Management Technology (16) Classics & World Religions (3) Communications Studies (2) Economics (8) English (21) Humanities (7) Finance (1) French (6) German (6) Spanish (6) Geography (2) Health Sciences (1) History (11) Human & Consumer Services (3) International Literature (2) Journalism (2) Law Enforcement Technology (4) Management (1) Marketing (2) Mathematics (13) Medical Assisting Technology (1) Music (2) Office Technology (3) Philosophy (6) Physical Education (2) Physical Science (3) Physics (6) Political Science (1) Professional Communication (1) Psychology (11) Quantitative Business Analysis (1) Sociology (6) Theater (3) Travel & Tourism (1) University College (3) Women's Studies (1)
Comments	VERY GOOD tuition rates. Great catalog materials. Only program in the nation specifically designed for prisoner-students. Staff is well aware of our unique challenges and will work with you to help you succeed. Extensive offerings in: Business Technology, Economics, English, History, Mathematics & Psychology. Unique offerings in aviation.

* The "ER" (Effective Rate) is factored for comparison to semester hours, and this rate covers ALL costs associated with registration including tuition, textbooks, supplies and lesson postage!

Oklahoma State University
Independent Study

309 Wes Watkins Center, Stillwater OK 74078-4061
800-522-4002 / 405-744-6390
osu.okstate.edu

Founded	Unknown (Catalog: 2007)
Accreditation	North Central Association of Colleges & Schools / UCEA
External Degree	None
Tuition	$115.00 credit hour / $67.86 fee per course (ER: $137.62)
Text Costs	Listed / No specific course bibliography
Time Limits	Maximum 12 months / 6-month extension $35.00 per credit hour enrolled
Transfer Hours	Non-Applicable
Curriculum	Accounting (2 courses) Animal Sciences (6) Anthropology (1) Business Administration (3) Business Communication (2) Communication Disorders (1) Communication Psychology (1) Economics (5) Electronics Technology (3) English (13) Educational Psychology (3) Finance (1) Fire Protection Safety Technology (10) French (3) Geography (7) Geology (1) German (2) Human Development, Family & Sexuality (3) Health (2) History (18) Horticulture (1) Journalism (1) Legal Small Business (2) Mathematics (9) Management (4) Marketing (2) MS-Computer (1) Music (1) Nutrition (1) Political Science (3) Psychology (2) Reference Measurement (1) Sociology (2) Statistics (7)
Comments	VERY GOOD tuition rates. Fair catalog. Incarcerated students. Extensive offerings in: English, Fire Protection Safety Technology, History, Mathematics, Statistics.

Oral Roberts University
School of Life Long Education

7777 South Lewis Avenue, Tulsa OK 74171
800-643-7976 / 918-495-6055
www.oru.edu

Founded	Unknown (Catalog: 2007)
Accreditation	North Central Association of Colleges & Schools / UCEA
External Degree	Bachelor of Science in: Business Administration, Christian Care & Counseling, Church Ministries, Liberal Studies/Arts (128 credits) Bachelor of Arts: Liberal Studies/Liberal Arts (128 credits) Minors: Bible, Christian Care & Counseling, Church History, Church Ministries, Evangelism & Missions, General Business, Liberal Studies, Theological Studies
Tuition	$225.00 credit hour / $20.00 fee per course (ER: $231.66)
Text Costs	Not Listed / Varies $60.00-$200.00 per course
Time Limits	Maximum 4 months / No info on extensions / Each course has three lessons & one exam
Transfer Hours	Yes. # not listed, but by means of transfer by accredited schools, examination (AP, CLEP, ORU, Faculty-Constructed Comprehensive Exams), prior learning assessments
Curriculum	Unknown / No course catalog sent with materials
Comments	AVERAGE tuition rates. Incomplete materials package. Application checklist includes: personal essay, signed honor code, minister's recommendation, and signed "Background Investigation Waiver."

Portland State University
Independent Study

P.O. Box 1491, Portland OR 97207-1491
800-547-8887 / 503-725-4865
www.pdx.edu

Founded	1997 (2007)
Accreditation	Northwest Association of Schools & Colleges
External Degree	None
Tuition	$101.00 per quarter credit hour / $20.00 per course registration fee (ER: $141.33)
Text Costs	Not listed / No bibliography
Time Limits	Minimum 1 month / Maximum 12 months / 6-month extension fee @ $30.00
Transfer Hours	Not Applicable / 2 Credit-By-Examination Courses @ ½ price
Curriculum	Criminology & Criminal Justice (3 courses) Chemistry (1) Economics (2) English (12) Geology (5) History (5) Mathematics (7) Psychology (4) Sociology (1)
Comments	VERY GOOD tuition rates. Adequate catalog. Incarcerated students. School offers nontraditional student scholarship for which some incarcerated individuals may be eligible.

Sam Houston State University
Correspondence Course Division

Box 2536, Huntsville TX 77341-2536
866-232-7528 / 936-294-1005
www.shsu.edu

Founded	1945 (Catalog: 2006-2007)
Accreditation	Southern Association of Colleges & Schools / NUCEA
External Degree	NONE
Tuition	$70.00 credit hour / $30.00 fee per course (ER: $80.00)
Text Costs	Not Listed
Time Limits	Maximum 1 year / 6-month extension @ $25.00
Transfer Hours	Non-Applicable
Curriculum	Accounting (2 courses) Agriculture (2) Art (1) Chemistry (4) Economics (3) English (12) Family & Consumer Sciences (4) Finance (3) General Business Administration (4) Geography (6) Health (3) History (6) Kinesiology (3) Management (2) Marketing (2) Mathematics (4) Philosophy (4) Photography (1) Political Science (2) Psychology (2) Sociology (6) Statistics (2)
Comments	EXCELLENT tuition rates. Adequate catalog. Incarcerated students. Several "Writing Enhanced" courses. Good school to wrack up a number of transferable hours to a higher-priced degree-graduating institution.

Seminary Extension

901 Commerce Street, Suite 500, Nashville TN 37203
800-229-4612 / 615-242-2453
www.seminaryextension.org

Founded	1951 (Catalog: 2007-2008)
Accreditation	Distance Education & Training Council / American Council on Education (ACE) College Credit Recommendation
External Degree	Certificate in Lay Ministry Training (ACE: 21 credit hours) Certificate in Bi-vocational Ministry (ACE: 24 credit course) Diplomas: Biblical Studies, Childhood Education, Christian Studies, Educational Ministries, Pastoral Ministries, (ACE: 48 credit hours) Advanced Diploma in Ministry (ACE: 96 credit hours)
Tuition	$28.00 per credit hour / $3.00 per ACE registration fee / $40.00 per course administration fee / $22.00 S&H per course (ER: $51.66) Complete 3 credit course packages less than $250.00
Text Costs	Listed / with bibliography
Time Limits	Maximum 6 months / 6-month extension for a fee
Transfer Hours	Maximum of 8 courses
Curriculum	Bible (1 course) Old Testament (6) New Testament (4) Theology (2) Christian Ethics (1) Church History (2) World Religion (1) Pastoral Ministries (4) Religious Education (2)
	*All 3000 numbered courses ACE-accredited 3 hours each
Comments	EXCELLENT tuition rates, however, be sure that ACE hours will be accepted by program you may intend to transfer to. Judson College will accept 30 hours from this program. Informative catalog but can be confusing. Incarcerated students. Basic level courses and programs available (see vocational section). Courses available in Spanish.

Southwest University

2200 Veterans Boulevard, Kenner LA 70062
800-433-5923 / 504-468-2900
www.southwest.edu

Founded	1982 (2007)
Accreditation	Distance Education & Training Council
External Degree	Certificates in: Criminal Justice (Intro & Advanced) / Human Resource Management / International Management / Leadership & Management / Management / Marketing / Organizational Management (12 credits) Associate of Science Business Administration (60 credits) Associate of Science Criminal Justice (60 credits) Bachelor of Science Criminal Justice (120 credits) Bachelor of Science Business Administration (120 credits) Concentrations: Human Resource Management / International Business / Leadership & Management / Marketing / Organizational Management
Tuition	$165.00 per credit hour (ER: $165.00)
Text Costs	$85.00 – $125.00 range + cost of study guides
Time Limits	13 weeks per course / 24 months for degree program / 1-month course extension @ $50.00 / 1-month degree program extension @ $10.00 per extension
Transfer Hours	30 credits per degree program / Life-Learning Portfolio Handbook available based on guides established by Council for Adult & Experiential Learning @ $60.00 per credit
Curriculum	Accounting (2 courses) Basic Mathematics & Statistics (3) Business (15) Communication (1) Criminal Justice (39) Economics (1) English (2) Finance (3) Human Relations (2) Human Resources Management (6) History (2) International Business (5)
	Management (7) Marketing (4) Organizational Management (2) Political Science (2) Psychology (1) Sociology (2)
Comments	GOOD tuition rates. Reasonable text prices, but suggest acquiring course bibliography and finding less expensive used texts from other sources. Due to the quick pace in which courses much be completed, this may not be a viable option if the administration at your institution is slow and lethargic. (Be sure of your "turn around" times). Allowed to retake final exams twice @ $50.00 fee. Honors program & Honor Society.

Texas State University-San Marcos
Office of Correspondence Studies

601 University Drive, San Marcos TX 78866
800-511-8656 / 512-245-2322
www.txstate.edu

Founded	1954 (Catalog: 2007-2008)
Accreditation	Southern Association of Colleges & Schools
External Degree	None
Tuition	$161.00
Text Costs	Not listed / Full bibliography
Time Limits	Maximum 9 months / Minimum 45 days / 3-month extension @$35.00
Transfer Hours	Non-Applicable
Curriculum	Art & Design (1 course) Biology (1) Business Law (1) Criminal Justice (1) Dance (1) English (13) Health Information Management (1) History (11) Mass Communication (1) Mathematics (7) Philosophy (2) Political Science (5) Psychology (7) Sociology (3) Spanish (5) Theater Arts (1)
Comments	GOOD tuition rates. Good catalog. Incarcerated students. Extensive offerings in: English.

Texas Tech University
Division of Outreach & Distance Education

Box 4219, Lubbock TX 79409-2191
800-692-6877 / 806-742-7200
www.ode.ttu.edu

Founded	1930 (2007 – 2008)
Accreditation	Southern Association of Colleges & Schools
External Degree	Bachelor of General Studies (120 credits) Areas of concentration: English / History / Psychology
Tuition	$143.67 per credit + $30.00 per course fee (ER: $153.67)
Text Costs	Not listed / Course bibliography included
Time Limits	6 months / 6-month extension @ $100.00
Transfer Hours	90 credits maximum / Credits by examination
Curriculum	Agriculture & Applied Economics (1 course) Business Administration (3) Economics (2) English (6) History (8) Human Development (5) Marketing (1) Mass Communication (4) Mathematics (8) Music (2) Nutritional Science (1) Plant & Soil Science (2) Political Science (2) Psychology (5) Restaurant & Hotel & Institutional Management (5 Spanish (2) Sociology, Anthropology & Social Work (2)
Comments	GOOD tuition rates. Good catalog, though tuition rates available only online. Incarcerated students. This would be a good school to transfer 90 credits compiled at lower tuition rates to complete a Baccalaureate degree. Structure of "General Studies" degree curriculum provides wide latitude for student to piece together requirements. Remember, a bachelor's degree in anything is better than no baccalaureate degree at all. This program, comparatively though, also exemplifies the negative effect of online programming growth versus correspondence offerings. There are fewer course offerings listed in this edition than in the second edition.

Thomas Edison State College

101 West State Street, Trenton NJ 08608-1176
888-442-8372
www.tesc.edu

Founded	1972 (Catalog: 2007-2008)
Accreditation	Middle States Association of Colleges & Schools
External Degree	Associate in Arts/Science: (60 hours) Applied Science / Applied Science & Technology (27 fields) Arts / Natural Science / Public & Social Services (10 fields) Bachelor of Arts / Science: (120 hours): Applied Science & Technology / Health Sciences (31 fields) Arts / Human Services (25 fields) Bachelor of Science in Business Administration (15 fields)
Tuition	No set rate with such an individualized program; would have to contact school & piece together degree
Text Costs	Not listed / Does not offer traditional correspondence courses
Time Limits	Non-Applicable
Transfer Hours	CORE OF SCHOOL: Prior Learning Assessment / ACE / CLEP / DANTES / TECEP / Military education & training programs / Professional accreditations & licenses honored
Curriculum	Thomas Edison State College Examination Program (TECEP) Business Management (23 tests) Computer Applications (1) Electrical/Electronic (2) English Composition (2) Humanities (8) Human Services (4) Natural Sciences/Mathematics (10) Social Sciences (19)
Comments	This is a non-traditional school for non-traditional students. The school is a national leader in evaluating knowledge acquired outside of the classroom for credit application towards degrees. If you have multiple-course credit completions, a myriad of life experiences, and/or military or professional training accomplishments, this would be a good place to coalesce all those credits into one or more accredited degrees. This, however, is by necessity an individualized program and thus very hard to convey the process in this outline format. The catalog, though, is more complicated and less informative than the version evaluated in the 2nd edition of this guide. A student investigating the viability of this program will have to contact the school's counselors beyond reviewing the catalog to determine if this program will work for them.

University of Arizona
Independent Study through Correspondence
Office of Continuing Education & Outreach

P.O. Box 210158, Tucson AZ 85721-0158
800-772-7480 / 520-626-4222
www.arizona.edu

Founded	1915 (Catalog: 2007-2008)
Accreditation	North Central Association of Colleges & Schools / UCEA
External Degree	None
Tuition	$252.00 / $15.00 per course fee
Text Costs	Listed (new & used) / Full bibliography
Time Limits	Maximum 9 months / 3-month extension @ $40.00 fee
Transfer Hours	Non-Applicable
Curriculum	Accounting (2 courses) American Indian Studies (3) Animal Sciences (1) Astronomy (1) Atmospheric Sciences (1) Chemistry (1) Civil Engineering (1) East Asia Studies (7) Family & Consumer Sciences (1) Family Studies & Human Development (3) French (7) Geography (2) Geosciences (1) German Studies (4) History (20) Italian (2) Judaic Studies (1) Mathematics (11) Near Eastern Studies (1) Pharmacology (1) Physics (2) Plant Pathology (1) Political Science (14) Psychology (21) Public Health (5) Renewable Natural Resources (1) Russian & Slavic Studies (6) Sociology (16) Traditions & Cultures (1)
Comments	ABOVE AVERAGE tuition rates. Good catalog. Incarcerated students. Extensive offerings in: East Asia Studies, French, History, Mathematics, Political Science, Psychology, Sociology.

University of Arkansas
Division of Continuing Education

2 East Center Street, Fayetteville AR 72701
800-638-1217 / 479-575-3647
http://istudy.uark.edu

Founded	Unknown (Catalog 2007)
Accreditation	North Central Association of Colleges & Schools
External Degree	None
Tuition	$99.99 residents / $7.00 course & $10.00 process fee (ER: $118.99) / $105.25 non-residents + $17.00 course fees (ER: $122.25)
Text Costs	Not listed / Full text bibliography in catalog
Time Limits	Minimum 6 weeks / Maximum 6 months / 6-month extension @ $40.00 / 3-month extension @ $40.00
Transfer Hours	Not-Applicable
Curriculum	Human Environmental Science (2) Anthropology (2) Biology (1) Criminal Justice (3) Drama (2) English (7) Foreign Languages: French (7) German (9) Spanish (2) Geography (5) History (6) Journalism (2) Mathematics (7) Philosophy (3) Political Science (3) Psychology (10) Social Work (1) Sociology (10) Office Systems Management (1) Education & Health Professionals (3) Health Kinesiology Recreation (10)
Comments	VERY GOOD tuition rates for both residents & non-residents. Plain but adequate catalog; missing enrollment forms though. Incarcerated students. Extensive offerings in Psychology, Sociology & Kinesiology.

University of Central Arkansas
Division of Academic
Outreach Extended Study Program

Brewer-Hegeman Conference Center, Suite 102, 201 Donaghey Avenue, Conway AR 72035
501-450-3118
www.uca-edu/aoep

Founded	1920 (2007 – 2008)
Accreditation	North Central Association of Colleges and Schools
External Degree	None
Tuition	$161.00 per credit + $38.50 in total fees per hour (ER: 199.50)
Text Costs	Not listed / No Bibliography Listed
Time Limits	Maximum 6 months / 6-month extension @ $120.00
Transfer Hours	Non-Applicable
Curriculum	Family & Consumer Science (1 course) Political Science (4) Health Sciences (2) History (5) Psychology (3) Sociology (2)
Comments	GOOD (barely) tuition rates. Good catalog. Incarcerated students.

University of Colorado at Boulder
Division of Continuing Education & Professional Studies

1505 University Avenue 178 UCB Boulder CO 80309-0178
800-331-2801 / 303-492-5148
www.colorado.edu

Founded	Unknown (2007-2008)
Accreditation	North Central Association of Colleges & Schools
External Degree	None
Tuition	$205.00 per credit hour (ER: $205.00)
Text Costs	Not Listed / No course bibliography
Time Limits	12 months / 12-month extension @ $60 per credit hour
Transfer Hours	Non-Applicable
Curriculum	Anthropology (2 courses) Economics (1) English (3) Geology (1) History (2) Mathematics (4) Philosophy (3) Political Science (3) Psychology (2) Sociology (1)
Comments	AVERAGE tuition rates. Adequate catalog. Incarcerated students. Correspondence Scholarships Program covers 80% of the cost of one course. Granted during Fall, Spring and Summer terms. Students must be enrolled in a course to be considered eligible.

"We are happy to work with a third party (such as a parent, spouse, or other person) who intends to help you coordinate your registration, payment, and scholarship application, if that makes the process easier."

University of Georgia
Center for Continuing Education

1197 South Lumpkin Street, Suite 193, Athens GA 30602-3603
800-877-3243 / 706-542-3243
www.uga.edu

Founded	Unknown (Catalog: 2007-2008)
Accreditation	Southern Association of Colleges & Schools
External Degree	NONE
Tuition	$171.00 (ER: $171.00)
Text Costs	Not Listed
Time Limits	Maximum 9 months / 3-month extension @ $60.00 fee
Transfer Hours	Non-Applicable
Curriculum	Agriculture (2-courses) Accounting (2) Anthropology (6) Application Turfgrass Management (1) Arts (1) Child & Family Development (4) Classics (3) Economics (5) English (9) Education Psychology (1) Food & Nutrition (2) French (4) Geography (2) Geology (2) History (7) Horticulture (4) Italian (2) Latin (2) Management (4) Mathematics (4) Music (2) Philosophy (4) Political Science (9) Psychology (5) Religion (3) Sociology (3) Spanish (5) Speech Communication (3) Women's Studies (1)
Comments	GOOD tuition rates Good catalog, even has section regarding prisoner enrollment (page 6). Incarcerated students. Extensive offerings in: English, Latin, Political Science.

University of Idaho
Independent Study

P.O. Box 443225, Moscow ID 83844-3225
877-464-3246 / 208-885-6641
www.uidaho.edu

Founded	1973 (Catalog: 2007)
Accreditation	Northwest Association of Colleges & Schools / AACIS
External Degree	None
Tuition	$100.00 per credit / $25.00 per course fee
Text Costs	Not Listed
Time Limits	Maximum 1 year / 6-month extension @ $75.00
Transfer Hours	Non-Applicable
Curriculum	Accounting (2 courses) Anthropology (5) Business (4) Business Law (1) Child & Family Studies (3) Economics (3) Education (4) English (8) Environmental Science (1) Family & Consumer Science (2) Finance (1) Health Care Administration (1) History (11) Library Science (13) Mathematics (6) Microbiology & Molecular Biology & Biochemistry (1) Musicology (2) Music History (2) Philosophy (3) Physics (5) Political Science (3) Psychology (12) Real Estate (3) Social Science (1) Sociology (4) Spanish (3)
Comments	VERY GOOD tuition rates. Good catalog. Incarcerated students. Extensive offerings in: History, Library Science & Psychology. Good school to complete multiple transferable hours to complete degree programs at more expensive schools.

University of Illinois at Urbana–Champaign
Guided Individual Study

Academic Outreach, Office of Continuing Education 302 East John Street, Suite 1406
Champaign IL 61820
800-252-1360 / 217-333-1320
www.uiuc.edu

Founded	Unknown (Catalog: 2007-2008)
Accreditation	North Central Association of Colleges & Schools
External Degree	None
Tuition	$240.00 per credit / $41 per credit & $30 course fee (ER: $291.00)
Text Costs	Not Listed
Time Limits	Maximum 9 months / Minimum 6 weeks / 3-month extension @ $100.00
Transfer Hours	Non-Applicable
Curriculum	Classical Civilization (1 course) English (2) French (4) German (2) History (2) Mathematics (5)
Comments	ABOVE AVERAGE tuition rates. Good catalog. Incarcerated students.

University of Kansas
Independent Study

1515 St. Andrews Drive, Lawrence KS 66047
877-404-5823 / 785-864-7894
www.ku.edu

Founded	1891 (Catalog Info: 2007-2008)
Accreditation	North Central Association of Colleges & Schools
External Degree	None
Tuition	$233.80 per credit hour / $50.00 per course fee (ER: $250.13)
Text Costs	Not listed
Time Limits	Maximum 9 months / 3-month extension @ $40.00 fee
Transfer Hours	Non-Applicable
Curriculum	Applied Behavioral Science (2) Art History (1) Biological Sciences (2) Classics (1) English (5) Geology (1) History (3) Humanities (2) Latin (3) Mathematics (6) Philosophy (2) Political Science (3) Psychology (4) Religious Studies (1) Sociology (1) Speech-Language-Hearing: Sciences & Disorders (1) Curriculum & Teaching (2) Educational Leadership & Policy Studies (1) Psychology & Research in Education (1) Musicology (1)
Comments	AVERAGE tuition rates. Good catalog. Incarcerated students enrolled.

University of Manitoba
Distance and Online Education

188D Extended Education Complex Winnipeg, Manitoba R3T 2N2 Canada
888-216-7011 – Canada
877-474-9420 – North America
www.umanitoba.ca

Founded	Unknown (Catalog: 2007-2008)
Accreditation	---------
External Degree	Bachelor of Arts: (3 year general degree) (90 hours) Majors: Canadian Studies / History / Political Science / Psychology / Minors: Anthropology / Canadian Studies / Economics / English / Geography / History / Philosophy / Political Studies / Psychology / Sociology
Tuition	$119.00 / $142.00 per credit hour depending on Faculty (ER: same) International students subject to 180% Differential Fee
Text Costs	Not listed / No bibliography
Time Limits	Maximum Term-based / Extensions unknown
Transfer Hours	Up to 42 credit hours towards BA degree
Curriculum	Faculty of Arts: Anthropology (5 courses) Classics (2) Economics (5) English (4) History (7) Native Studies (2) Philosophy (3) Political Studies (5) Psychology (15) Religion (3) Sociology (8) Faculty of Environment, Earth & Resources: Environment & Geography (8) Geological Sciences (4) Faculty of Education: Educational Administration, Foundations & Psychology (7) Faculty of Human Ecology: Family & Social Sciences (1) Faculty of Nursing: Nursing (6) Faculty of Physical Education & Recreation Studies: Physical Education (1) Faculty of Science: Biology (2) Mathematics (3) Microbiology (1) Faculty of Social Work: Social Work (9) School of Arts: Art (3)
Comments	VERY GOOD tuition rates for citizens to AVERAGE for non-citizens. Confusing to complicated catalog. Incarcerated students. Another example of shift towards online programming that is decreasing distance education opportunities for prisoners.

University of Minnesota
College of Continuing Education

20 Classroom Office Building, 1994 Buford Avenue, St. Paul MN 55108
800-234-6564 / 612-624-4000
www.cce.umn.edu

Founded	Unknown (Catalog: 2007-2008)
Accreditation	North Central Association of Colleges & Schools
External Degree	NONE
Tuition	Not Listed in Catalog resident/nonresident status (ER: Unknown) Senior Citizen (62+) Discount = $10 per credit for residents / $82.50 IDL fee (2-5 credits) + $48.75 per credit fee
Text Costs	Not listed / No bibliographical listing either
Time Limits	Maximum 9 months / Possible extension
Transfer Hours	Non-Applicable
Curriculum	Afro-American Studies (1 course) Agronomy & Plant Genetics (1) Art History (1) Biology (2) Child Psychology (2) Ecology, Evolution, & Behavior (1) Economics (2) Educational Psychology (1) English Composition (4) English Literature (10) Finance (1) Food Science & Nutrition (1) French (3) Genetics, Cell Biology & Development (1) Geology & Geophysics (2) Journalism & Mass Communication (4) Latin (2) Mathematics (7) Music (2) Norwegian (1) Nursing (2) Occupational Therapy (1) Philosophy (1) Physics (3) Post Secondary Teaching & Learning (10) Psychology (1) Russian (2) Spanish (4) Swedish (2)
Comments	UNKOWN tuition rates. Essentially a poor catalog. Extensive offerings in: English Literature.

University of Mississippi
Independent Study

P.O. Box 729, University MS 38677-0729
662-915-7313
www.olemiss.edu

Founded	Unknown (Catalog: 2007-2008)
Accreditation	Southern Association of Colleges & Schools
External Degree	None
Tuition	$180 per credit hour (ER: $180.00)
Text Costs	Not listed
Time Limits	Maximum 12 months / Minimum 2 months
Transfer Hours	Non-Applicable
Curriculum	Accounting (3 courses) Art (2) Biology (2) Business Administration (1) Chemistry (3) Criminal Justice (3) Economics (1) Education-Curriculum & Instruction (1) Education-Elementary Education (1) Education-Library Science (1) Education-Special Education (1) Education-Reading Education (4) Education-Counseling & Educational Psychology (3) English (10) Family & Consumer Sciences (2) Finance (3) Languages: French (4) German (4) Portuguese (4) Spanish (4) History (2) Health Promotion (3) Journalism (1) Legal Studies (2) Library Science (1) Marketing (3) Mathematics (2) Park & Recreation Management (3) Philosophy (6) Religion (3) Telecommunications (1) Wellness (1)
Comments	GOOD tuition rates. Flashy catalog. Incarcerated students. Extensive offerings in: Education & English. Students must have access to standard audiotape player/recorder.

University of Missouri
Center for Distance Education & Independent Study

136 Clark Hall, Columbia MO 65211-4200
800-609-3727 / 573-882-2491
www.missouri.edu

Founded	1911 (Catalog: 2007-2008)
Accreditation	North Central Association of Colleges & Schools / AACIS
External Degree	None
Tuition	$235.90 per credit / $11.70 per credit fee (ER: $247.60)
Text Costs	Listed with full bibliography
Time Limits	Maximum 9 months / 3-month extension @ $35.00
Transfer Hours	Non-Applicable
Curriculum	Accountancy (2 courses) Anthropology (2) Astronomy (2) Atmospheric Sciences (1) Biological Engineering (1) Black Studies (1) Classical Studies: Latin (2) Economics (5) Education: Career Planning (1) Education: Learning, Teaching & Curriculum (4) Engineering (2) English: Composition & Creative Writing (2) English: Language (1) English: Literature (13) Geography (2) Geological Sciences (1) History (4) Management (1) Mathematics (6) Philosophy (3) Physical Education (1) Psychology (2) Romance Languages: French (2) Spanish (1) Women's & Gender Studies (1)
Comments	AVERAGE tuition rates. Good catalog. Extensive offerings in English.

University of Nebraska-Lincoln
Extended Education & Outreach
College of Independent Study

900 North 22nd Street, Lincoln NE 68588-8802
866-700-4747 (Toll Free) / 402-472-2175
www.unl.edu

Founded	1915 (Catalog: 2007-2008)
Accreditation	North Central Association of Colleges & Schools
External Degree	None
Tuition	$192.25 credit hour / $105.00 fees per course (ER: $227.25)
Text Costs	Listed / Titles & ISBN's / Syllabus $15-$45
Time Limits	Maximum 12 months / 3-month extension @ $65.00
Transfer Hours	Non-Applicable
Curriculum	Accounting (1 course) Art & Art History (1) Biological Sciences (1) Business Law (1) Child, Youth, & Family Studies (1) Classics (1) Economics (4) English (5) Finance (3) Geography (3) History (6) Industrial & Management Systems Engineering (1) Journalism (1) Management (6) Marketing (1) Mathematics (3) Nutrition Sciences (1) Physics & Astronomy (4) Political Science (5) Psychology (2) Sociology (4)
Comments	AVERAGE tuition rates. Good catalog. Incarcerated students.

University of Nevada, Reno
Independent Learning

Continuing Education Bldg, 1041 North Virginia Street, Reno NV 89557
800-233-8928 / 775-784-4046
www.unr.edu

Founded	Unknown (Catalog: 2007)
Accreditation	Commission on Colleges of the Northwest Association
External Degree	None via correspondence / all online
Tuition	$125.00 credit hour / $60.00 fees per course (ER: $145.00)
Text Costs	Listed with full bibliography & cost
Time Limits	Maximum 1 year / Minimum 4 weeks / 6-month extension @ $75.00 fee
Transfer Hours	Non-Applicable
Curriculum	Anthropology (2 courses) Counseling & Educational Psychology (1) English (6) Foreign Languages: Basque (4) French (4) German (4) Italian (4) Spanish (2) Health Ecology (1) History (5) Mathematics (9) Music (1) Nutrition (1) Political Science (3) Psychology (1)
Comments	VERY GOOD tuition rates. Good informative catalog. Incarcerated students. Extensive offerings in Mathematics & Foreign Languages with unique offering in Basque.

University of North Carolina
Center for Continuing Education

Campus Box 1020, Chapel Hill NC 27599-1020
800 862-5669 / 919 962-1134
www.unc.edu

Founded	1913 (Catalog 2007)
Accreditation	Southern Association of Colleges & Schools (UCEA)
External Degree	None
Tuition	$117.00 per credit + 9.00 fee – Resident (ER: $126.00) / $250.00 per credit + 9.00 fee – Nonresident (ER:$259.00) / $117.00 per credit by Examination test – Residents (ER: $39.00) / $250.00 per credit by Examination test – Nonresidents (ER: $83.33)
Text Costs	Not listed / Bibliography in catalog
Time Limits	Maximum 9 months / Minimum 12 weeks / 1st 4-month extension @ $30.00 / 2nd 4-month extension @ $75.00
Transfer Hours	Not-Applicable
Curriculum	Accounting (1 course) African Studies (1) Anthropology (1) Art (2) Biology (2) Chemistry (4) Classics (2) Economics (2) English (12) Geography (3) History (12) Hospitality (1) Italian (4) Latin (1) Mathematics (8) Music (1) Nursing (1) Philosophy (1) Political Science (3) Psychology (2) Russian (1) Sociology (7) Spanish (5) Statistics (2)
Comments	VERY GOOD in-state tuition rates. HIGH rates for nonresidents. Good catalog materials. "UNC-Chapel Hill participates in several programs designed to assist persons in the NC prison system who are interested in pursuing college level work. Outreach to inmates (800-862-5669) enables qualified inmates to enroll in correspondence courses at no charge." For in-state prisoner-students there is no better deal to accumulate transferable credit hours for degree completions elsewhere. If the Credit by Examination option is viable for you, UNC is an excellent value.

University of North Dakota
Division of Continuing Education

Gustafson Hall – Room 103, 3264 Campus Road Stop 902, Grand Forks ND 58202-9021
800-342-8230 / 701-777-2661
www.und.edu

Founded	1910 (Catalog 2007-2008)
Accreditation	North Central Association of Colleges & Schools / UCEA
External Degree	Bachelor of Arts in Social Sciences (125 hours) Bachelor of General Studies (125 hours)
Tuition	$120.00 credit hour / $40.00 fee per course (ER: 139.33) / University degree program admissions fee $35.00
Text Costs	Not Listed
Time Limits	Maximum 9 months / 3-month extension @ $35.00
Transfer Hours	Yes: up to 95 semester credit hours
Curriculum	Anthropology (2 courses) Art (3) Chemical Engineering (1) Communication (2) English (4) Fine Arts (1) French (3) Geology (2) History (5) Mathematics (9) Music (1) Psychology (3) Teaching & Learning (2)
Comments	VERY GOOD tuition rates. Good & informative catalog. Incarcerated students. Interlibrary loan program. Reasonably well organized program, fair price, but with relatively limited correspondence course selection, many transfer hours will be required for degree completion. Might be good program to transfer the maximum allowable hours (less costly credits earned elsewhere) to fulfill degree requirements.

University of Northern Iowa
Guided Independent Study

2637 Hudson Road, Cedar Falls IA 50614-0223
800-772-1746 / 319-273-2123
www.uni.edu

Founded	Unknown (2007 – 2008)
Accreditation	North Central Association of Colleges & Schools
External Degree	Certificate in Criminology (18 credits) Bachelor of Liberal Studies (124 credits)
Tuition	$174.00 per credit hour + $13.00 per course fee
Text Costs	Not Listed / No Bibliography
Time Limits	Minimum 6 weeks / Maximum 9 months / 3-month extension @ $15.00
Transfer Hours	Mandatory minimum 62 credit hours for BLS / Maximum unknown
Curriculum	Accounting (2 courses) Communication Studies (2) Design, Textiles, Gerontology & Family Studies (4) Education – Elementary & Middle Level (3) Health Promotion & Education (1) Leisure Services (1) Literacy (1) Physical Education (1) Social Foundations (1) Post Secondary Student Affairs (1) Psychology (2) English language & Literature (2) Geography (1) Humanities (4) Marketing (1) Mathematics (2) Music (2) Religion (2) Social Science (1) Social Work (3) Sociology & Criminology (9)
Comments	GOOD tuition rates. Good catalog. Incarcerated students. Extensive offerings in education. Interesting certificate program and possibly a school to consider for degree consolidation.

University of Saskatchewan
Centre for Continuing & Distance Education

237 Williams Bldg, 221 Cumberland Ave North
Saskatoon SK S7N 1 M3 Canada
866-966-5563
www.usask.ca/

Founded	Unknown (Catalog: 2007-2008)
Accreditation	Unknown
External Degree	Certificate Program in Teaching English as a Second Language (6 courses of one of two streams of study)
Tuition	$146.00 to $228.00 per credit hour (ER: ssame) Non-resident rates 1.5 times resident rate / Senior citizen (65+) tuition waiver program
Text Costs	Not listed / No bibliography in catalog
Time Limits	Term-based / Extensions not listed
Transfer Hours	Not Listed
Curriculum	Anthropology (1 course) Archaeology (1) Economics (2) English (4) Geography (5) Geology (2) History (2) Native Studies (1) Psychology (3) Religion (1) Sociology (10) Women's Studies (1)
Comments	Variable tuition rates depending on particular course & resident status: with present exchange rates, not a good buy for non-residents. So-so catalog. Extensive offerings in Sociology.

University of South Carolina
Distance Education

P.O. Box 2346, Columbia SC 29202-2346
800-922-2577 / 803-777-7210
http://learn.sc.edu

Founded	1801 (Catalog Info: 2005-2006)
Accreditation	Southern Association of Colleges & Schools
External Degree	None – National Universities Degree Consortium (NUDC)
Tuition	$125.00 per credit hour / $40 per course fee (ER: $138.33)
Text Costs	Not Listed
Time Limits	Maximum 12 months / 3-month extension @ $35.00 fee
Transfer Hours	Non-Applicable
Curriculum	Accounting (10) Astronomy (4) Economics (6) English (15) Finance (4) Geography (4) Health Promotion, Education & Behavior (2) History (10) Latin (2) Management (2) Marine Science (1) Marketing (3) Mathematics (7) Music (1) Philosophy (2) Political Science (1) Psychology (9) Social Work (7) Statistics (1)
Comments	VERY GOOD tuition rates. Good catalog. Extensive offerings in: Accounting, English, History, Psychology & Social Work. NUDC member schools facilitate completion of several degree programs via Colorado State, Kansas State, Washington State & Weber State Universities & Universities of Alabama & Houston. This means USC credits are readily transferable to these & other programs.

University of South Dakota
Division of Continuing Education
Correspondence Division

414 East Clark Street, Vermillion SD 57069
800-233-7937 / 605-677-6240
www.usd.edu

Founded	Unknown (Catalog Info: Fall 2007)
Accreditation	Northwest Association of Colleges & Schools
External Degree	None via correspondence / Multiple (17) via online programming
Tuition	$203.00 per credit hour
Text Costs	Not Listed / USD Barnes & Noble Bookstore only source for correspondence guides
Time Limits	Maximum Standard courses follow standard academic calendar / Non-Standard courses allow 350 days for completion with 60-day extensions approved on case-by-case basis & $50.00 extension fee
Transfer Hours	Non-Applicable
Curriculum	Alcohol & Drug Abuse Studies (5) American Indian Art History (1) Anthropology (2) Art Education (1) Art History (5) Criminal Justice (9) Elementary Education (1) English (8) Education Psychology (1) Geography (1) General Fine Arts (1) History (6) Health (2) Indian Studies (1) Mathematics (4) Mass Communication (3) Political Science (3) Religion (3) Sociology (19) Statistics (1) Theater (2)
Comments	AVERAGE tuition rates. Extensive offerings in Criminal Justice & Sociology. Could use some informative true correspondent student-oriented catalog.

University of Wisconsin - Plattesville
Distance Learning Center

1 University Plaza, Plattesville WI 53818-3099
800-362-5460 / 608-342-1468
www.uwplatt.edu

Founded	1978 (Catalog: 2007-2008)
Accreditation	North Central Association of Colleges & Schools
External Degree	Certificate in: Leadership & Human Performance / Human Resourses / Management / International Business / Marketing (9 credits) Bachelor of Science in Business Administration (120 credits) Major – Business Administration / Minor – Accounting
Tuition	$200.80 per credit for Wisconsin Resident (ER: $220.80) $516.34 per credit hour for Nonresident (ER: $536.34) $10.00 per credit fee / $30.00 per course fee / $35.00 application fee
Text Costs	Not Listed
Time Limits	Maximum 12 months / One extension @ $30.00
Transfer Hours	Maximum 88 credit hours / Portfolio $75.00 assessment fee + $150.00 (1-9 credits) $50.00 credit beyond transcription fee
Curriculum	Accounting (8 courses) Business Administration (27) Communication (1) Computer Science (1) Economics (3) Mathematics (1) Music (1) Speech (1)
Comments	AVERAGE to SKY HIGH tuition rates. So-so catalog. Incarcerated students. Extensive offerings in: Business Administration. A fair program if you are a state resident & business is your focus. Suggest maximum transferrable hours, though, from other less expensive schools.

University of Wisconsin
Independent Learning

505 South Rosa Road, Suite 200, Madison WI 53719-1277
877-895-3276 / 608-262-2011

Founded	1892 (one of the nation's original distance education universities) (Catalog: 2007-2008)
Accreditation	North Central Association of Colleges & Schools
External Degree	None
Tuition	$199 per credit hour / $60 administration fee (ER: $219)
Text Costs	Not Listed / Bibliography (text/author/publication date)
Time Limits	Maximum 12 months / 3-month extension @ $25
Transfer Hours	Non-Applicable
Curriculum	African American Studies (1 course) African Languages & Literature (1) Agricultural Economics (1) Anthropology (3) Art (1) Art History (2) Astronomy (1) Botany (1) Business (3) Law (2) Management (6) Marketing (1) Chemistry (2) Classics (2)
	Exceptional (2) Child & Family Studies (1) Counseling Psychology (1) Curriculum & Instruction (4) Educational Policy Studies (1) Educational Psychology (10) Technical Communication Series (7) English (24) French (15) Geography (2) Geology (1) German (7) Greek (2) Health Education (1) Hebrew & Semitic Studies (6) History (9) Italian (2) Latin (5) Mathematics (10) Meteorology (1) Music (5) Philosophy (4) Physics (2) Political Science (1) Portuguese (2) Psychology (4) Russian (4) Sociology (7) Spanish (12) Statistics (1)
Comments	AVERAGE tuition rates. Good comprehensive catalog. Incarcerated students. Extensive offerings in: Educational Psychology, English, French, History, Mathematics & Spanish. Check out vocational listing for Disaster Management & CEU courses.

University of Wisconsin
Independent Study

505 South Rosa Road Suite 200, Madison WI 53719-1277
877-895-3276 / 608-262-2011

Program	Certificate of Completion
Founded	1892 (one of the nation's original distance education programs)
Accreditation	North Central Association of Colleges & Schools
External Degree	No
Tuition	$95.00 / $207 per course + $50/5.00 admission fee (1.0/5.0 CEUs) (some courses count significantly more & offer many more CEUs)
Text Costs	Bibliography & materials listed
Time Limits	Maximum 12 months / 3-month extension @ $25.00
Transfer Hours	Non-Applicable
Curriculum	Agricultural Economics (1 course) Art (1) Business (4) Law (2) Management (6) Marketing (1) Personal/Professional Business Development (2) Disaster Management (13) English (2) French (2) Health (1) Health Education (1) Italian (1) Mathematics (2) Polish (3) Russian (1) Writing (1) A myriad of subject offerings, where the student can earn continuing education units (CEUs) for each course. One CEU is generally defined as the equivalent of ten contact hours of participation in an organized continuing education experience under qualified instruction.
Comments	GOOD tuition rates. Good catalog. Interesting well-designed courses. Extensive offering in Disaster Management; be sure to check out that Diploma program.

University of Utah
Distance Education

1901 E. South Campus Drive Room 1215, Salt Lake City UT 84112
800-467-8839 / 801-581-8801
www.continue.utah.edu/distance

Founded	1925 (Catalog: unknown)
Accreditation	Northwest Association of Colleges & Schools
External Degree	None
Tuition	Unknown
Text Costs	Not Listed
Time Limits	Unknown
Transfer Hours	Non-Applicable
Curriculum	Anthropology (2 courses) Art (1) Biology (2) Chemistry (2) Economics (5) English (5) Finance (1) History (4) Math (7) Music (2) Nutrition (1) Physics (5) Political Science (3) Psychology (9) Special Education (1) Teaching & Learning (10)
Comments	Unknown tuition rates. Pitiful catalog/materials as evidenced by the lack of information available in this profile. Extensive offerings in: Psychology and Teaching & Learning.

Upper Iowa University
External Degree Program

P.O. Box 1861, Fayette IA 52142
888-877-3742 / 563-425-5252
www.uiu.edu

Founded	1973 (Catalog 2007-2008)
Accreditation	North Central Association of Colleges & Schools
External Degree	Certificates: Emergency & Disaster Management (15 credits) Human Resources Management, Marketing, Organizational Communication, Organizational Leadership / Associates of Arts: Liberal Arts / General Business (60 credits) Bachelor of Science: 17 Majors & 13 Minors! (120 credits)
Tuition	254.00 per credit hour (ER: $254.00)
Text Costs	Not Listed
Time Limits	Maximum 6 months / 6-month extension @ $50.00
Transfer Hours	AA 45 credits & BS 90 credits / ACE / CLEP / DSST / Experiential Learning Credit (packet includes compilation process brochure!)
Curriculum	Art (1 course) Biology (1) Business Administration (45) Communications (2) Criminal Justice (9) English (3) Health Services Administration (4) Interdisciplinary (4) Management Information Systems (1) Mathematics (5) Physical Science (1) Political Science/Public Administration (10) Psychology (18) Religion (1) Sociology (6)
Comments	AVERAGE tuition rates. Good catalog & great packet. Incarcerated students. Extensive Degree offerings, perhaps the most expansive correspondence program available,. It has the most majors & minors that I have come across. Extensive offerings in: Business Administration, Criminal Justice, Political Science/Public Administration, Psychology. Dean's List & Graduation academic honors program. Good option to earn/compile transfer credits and complete degree program.

Vincennes University
Division of Continuing Studies

1002 North First Street, Vincennes IN 47591
812-888-5900 / 800-880-7961
www.vinu.edu

Founded	1801 (Catalog 2007)
Accreditation	North Central Association of Colleges & Schools
External Degree	Certificates of Program Completion: 5 options / Associate in Arts: 4 options / Associate of Applied Sciences: 7 options / Associate of Science: 11 options
Tuition	$144.66 (ER: $144.66)
Text Costs	Not listed / No bibliography in catalog
Time Limits	Maximum 1 year / 6-month extension @ $50.00
Transfer Hours	Yes: CLEP/ DANTES / Life Experience Credit, etc.
Curriculum	Accounting (2 courses) Management (2) Office Administration (4) Corrections (1) Law Enforcement (4) Fitness (1) English (3) Humanities (1) Speech (2) Economics (1) History (3) Political Science (2) Psychology (2) Sociology (1) Earth Science (1) Mathematics (1)
Comments	VERY GOOD tuition rates. Poor catalog materials. Incarcerated students. Most distance education courses are online. Does not appear possible to earn enough credits directly from this school to complete degree requirements, thus transfer credits will be required.

Western Washington University Independent Learning

516 High Street – MS 5293, Bellingham WA 98225-5996
360-650-3650
www.wwu.edu

Founded	Unknown (Catalog: 2006)
Accreditation	Northwest Association of Colleges & Schools / AACIS
External Degree	None
Tuition	$95.00 per credit / $20.00 per course fee (ER: $102.33)
Text Costs	Not Listed
Time Limits	Maximum 9 month / 3-month extension @ $35.00
Transfer Hours	Non-Applicable
Curriculum	Anthropology (4 courses) Classical Studies (1) Communication (1) Decision Sciences (1) East Asia Studies (7) Economics (4) Engineering Technology (1) English (21) Environmental Science (2) Environmental Studies (4) Greek (1) History (4) Latin (1) Liberal Studies (2) Library Science (1) Management Information Systems (1) Mathematics (5) Mongolian (3) Music (1) Psychology (3) Sociology (5) Women's Studies (1)
Comments	VERY GOOD tuition rates (though have probably gone up by publication date). Good catalog. Incarcerated students. Extensive to unique offerings in: East Asia Studies, English, Mongolian & selection of "Writing Proficiency Course." Student could accumulate a lot of transferable credit hours for a very good price at this school.

Graduate Program Outlines

Atlantic University

215 67th Street, Virginia Beach VA 23451-8101
800-428-1512 / 757-631-8101
www.atlantic-university.org

Founded	1985 (Catalog: 2006-2008)
Accreditation	Distance Education & Training Council / International Association for Continuing Education & Training
External Degree	Master of Arts in Transpersonal Studies* (37 credits)
Tuition	$231.66 credit hour / $85.00 fee per course (ER: $260.00) / Application fee $50.00/ Diploma fee $75.00
Text Cost	Not Listed / Study guides & materials supplied with surcharge
Time Limits	Not Listed
Transfer Hours	Yes: 6 credit hours
Curriculum	Transpersonal Studies (15 courses) / Health & Mental Therapy (10) / Inner Spirituality (8) / Leadership & Peace Building (5) / Transpersonal Hypnosis (3) / Visual Arts & Transpersonal (5) / Creative Writing & Transpersonal (4) / Others (7)
Comments	GOOD tuition rates. Different kind of program and thus a bit different kind of catalog. Incarcerated students. Scholarship for students designated "with unconditional status and have earned at least six credit hours from AU."

*Transpersonal Studies is an inter-disciplinary approach to understanding human nature and the world around us. TS seeks to blend critical and contemplative thinking. The Transpersonal researcher maintains a fundamental appreciation for the value of human experience itself as meaningful research data.

California Coast University

700 North Main Street, Santa Ana CA 92701
888-228-8648 / 714-547-9625
www.calcoast.edu

Founded	1973 (Catalog 2007-2008)
Accreditation	Distance Education & Training Council*
External Degree	Master of Business Administration – Business Administration / Human Resources Management (39 credits) Master of Education – Administration / Curriculum & Instruction (36 credits) Master of Science – Psychology (39 credits) (all degrees with option of with or without thesis)
Tuition	$210.00 per credit hour [Continental US] (ER: $210.00) $240.00 per credit hour [Outside Continental U.S.] (ER: $240.00) (Tuition Payment Plan Available)
Text Cost	Not Listed / No Bibliography / Textbook rental program
Time Limits	Minimum 9 months for degree / Maximum 5 years for degree
Transfer Hours	Maximum 6 credits
Curriculum	Business Administration (12 courses) Education (15 courses) Graduate Methodology [i.e., thesis courses (3 courses) Psychology (12 courses)
Comments	GOOD tuition rates. Catalog explains program well. This school is structured to serve the more life-experienced and self-starting student. CCU courses encompass a study guide with recommended texts and a self-study outline. Timed exams are proctored with "students permitted to utilize any notes, study guides, calculators or other material used during the completion of their course work" (p.6 catalog). NOTE: From experience this is not as easy as it seems. Costs are reasonable, DETC-accredited (though credits may not be readily transferable to other state-supported schools?); this could be a good option for the prisoner-student to earn a recognized graduate degree.

*"Credits and degrees earned through CCU are recognized for promotions, assignments, and position qualification standards, within the US military and Federal government" (p.3 catalog).

Catholic Distance University

120 East Colonial Highway, Hamilton VA 20158
888-254-4CDU / 540-338-2700
www.cdu.edu

Founded	1983 (2007-2008)
Accreditation	Distance Education & Training Council
External Degree	Master of Arts in Theology (39 credits)
Tuition	$369.00 per credit hour (ER: $369.00) $150.00 annual technology fee; will increase ER rate.
Text Cost	Average $60.00 / Course bibliography listed. Catechism of the Catholic Church & Catholic Bible required for all courses.
Time Limits	3 to 6 months / Extension @ full tuition fee / 5 years to complete degree program
Transfer Hours	6 credits for BA program
Curriculum	Church and Theology (29 courses)
Comments	HIGH tuition rates. Good text prices. Good catalog. Incarcerated students. Highly focused degree program. Opportunity to qualify for Delta Epsilon Tau: International Honor Society for Distance Learning. NOTE: course materials shipped in 3-ring binders thus you may need to make special arrangements due to your facility's property restrictions.

Colorado State University
Division of Continuing Education

Spruce Hall 1040 Campus Delivery, Fort Collins CO 80523-1040
877-491-4336 / 970-491-5288
www.colostate.edu

Founded	1967 (Catalog: 2007-2008)
Accreditation	North Central Association of Colleges & Schools
External Degree	None via correspondence / All online
Tuition	Not Listed - varies
Text Cost	Not Listed
Time Limits	Maximum 6 months / 6-month extension
Transfer Hours	Non-Applicable
Curriculum	Business (16 courses) (DVD)*/ Civil Engineering (5) (DVD)*/ Education (3) (Videotape set)*/ Food Science & Human Nutrition (1) (Correspondence) / Fishery & Wildlife Biology (2) (Correspondence) / Natural Resources (2) (Correspondence) / Natural Resources Recreation & Tourism (1) (Correspondence)
Comments	UNKNOWN tuition rates. Another school that has nearly phased out correspondence study. Catalog can be confusing and not as informative as it should be. Prisoners may be eligible for "John C Snider" and "Colorado Commission on Higher Education Extended Studies" Scholarships. Contact school for requirements.

* NOTE: DVD & Videotape set courses require electronics that all prisoners may not have access to. Additionally, these courses may also require internet access; CSU's catalog is not clear about this.

Global University School of Graduate Studies

1211 South Glenstone Avenue, Springfield MO 65804
800-443-1083 / 417-862-9533
www.globaluniversity.edu

Founded	1948 (2008)
Accreditation	Distance Education & Training Council
External Degree	Master of Arts in Biblical Studies (36 credits) Master of Arts in Ministerial Studies (36 Credits) Master of Divinity (90 Credits)
Tuition	$195.00 per credit hour / 20% prisoner-student discount (ER: $156.00)
Text Cost	$120.00 average per course / Separate bibliography catalog
Time Limits	6 months / 1-year extension @ $25.00 fee
Transfer Hours	9 credits for Master of Arts program / 21 credits for Master of Divinity program
Curriculum	Bible Studies (16 courses) New Testament (9 courses) Old Testament (4 courses) Ministerial Education (7 courses) Ministerial Leadership (3 courses) Ministries (3 courses) Missions (9 courses) Practical Theology (6 courses) Research (3 courses) Theology (4 courses)
Comments	EXCELLENT tuition rates. Good informative materials. Welcoming program for prisoner-students, and has been so for quite some time. Delta Epsilon Tau Honor Society chapter. Highly focused degree program designed for distance education delivery. Specific counselor assigned to prisoner-students.

Huntington College of Health Sciences

1204-D Kenesaw, Knoxville TN 37919
800-290-4226 / 865-524-8079
www.hchs.edu

Founded	1985 (Catalog 2007)
Accreditation	Distance Education & Training Council / International Association for Continuing Education & Training
External Degree	Master of Science in Nutrition (thesis option) (35 credits) / Master of Science in Nutrition (non-thesis option) (37 credits)
Tuition	$350.00 per course for non-matriculated students (ER: $350.00) / $285.00 per course for program enrolled students (ER: $285.00) / $9,870.00 M.S. with thesis option (ER: $183.33) / $10,440.00 M.S. non-thesis option (ER: $183.33) (Tuition payment plan available)
Text Cost	Master of Science - thesis option ($1,075) / Master of Science- non-thesis option ($1,340) (estimated cost of textbooks, materials, S&H per program)
Time Limits	Maximum 4 months per course / 3-month extension @ $50.00 / Master Degree program 36 months
Transfer Hours	Maximum 18 credit hours
Curriculum	Chemistry (1 course) / Nutritional Sciences (12 courses)
Comments	AVERAGE to HIGH tuition rates. Good catalog; though no course text bibliographies ("available via website" / you will need to write). Incarcerated students. Extensive offerings in: Nutrition Science. Many well paying health care industry positions such as these programs are available to ex-felons. If this field is of interest, check out this school.

Newport University

4101 Westerly Place, Suite #103, Newport Beach CA 92660
949-757-1155
www.newport.edu

Founded	1976 (2007 – 2008)
Accreditation	Approved by the State of California, Bureau of Private Post-Secondary & Vocational Education
External Degree	Master of Arts in Business Administration (30 credits) / Master of Arts in Human Behavior (30 credits) / Master of Arts in Psychology (39 credits) / Doctorate in Human Behavior (90 credits)
Tuition	$159.00 per credit MA Program (ER $169.00) / $170.00 per credit PhD Program (ER $170.00) / $2500 Dissertation Committee Review fee / $100.00 Application fee
Text Cost	Not listed / No Bibliography in catalog
Time Limits	Satisfactory progress requires 2 course completions per year
Transfer Hours	Up to 6-12 credits in MA program / 39 credits PhD program / Life Experience Credits
Curriculum	MA Business Administration Core Courses (6) Electives (30) MA Human Behavior Core Courses (13) Electives (5) MA Psychology Core Courses (13) Electives (7) PhD Human Behavior Prerequisite (10) Core Courses (16)
Comments	EXCELLENT tuition rates. So-so catalog materials. Incarcerated students. If no other options are applicable, and all other aspects are considered, an MA/PhD from this school is better than none. This is not a "diploma mill".
	Grants of $300.00 – $500.00 per year possible, determined at time of enrollment evaluation. "If Licensing is the ultimate goal of the student, the University strongly advises their students to check with their respective state, school district or professional associations for specific requirements" (page 5 of catalog)

Southwest University

2200 Veterans Boulevard, Kenner, LA 70062 504-468-2900
800-433-5923
www.southwest.edu

Founded	1982 (2007)
Accreditation	Distance Education & Training Council
External Degree	Certificates in Business Administration (12 credits) / Leadership & Management / Management / Organizational Management / Criminal Justice / Master of Arts in Organizational Management (36 credits) / Master of Business Administration (36 credits) / Master of Science in Criminal Justice (36 credits)
Tuition	$250.00 per credit hour (ER: $165.00)
Text Cost	$85.00 – $125.00 range + cost of study guides
Time Limits	13 weeks per course / 24 months for degree program / 1-month course extension @ $50.00 / 1 month degree program extension @ $10.00 per extension.
Transfer Hours	9 credits per degree program / Life-Learning Portfolio Handbook available based on guides established by Council for Adult & Experiential Learning @ $60.00 per credit
Curriculum	Accounting (1 course) Criminal Justice (13) Decision Process (1) Economics (1) Finance (1) Human Resource Management (2) Management (4) Management Business Administration (4) Marketing (1) Organizational Management (3)
Comments	GOOD/AVERAGE Tuition rates. Reasonable text prices, but suggest acquiring course bibliography and seeking less expensive used texts from other sources. Due to the quick pace in which courses must be completed, this may not be a viable option if the administration at your institution is slow and lethargic. (Be sure of your "turn around" times). Allowed to retake final exams twice @ $50.00 fee. Honors Program & Honor Society

Texas State University–San Marcos
Office of Correspondence Studies
601 University Drive, San Marcos TX 78866
800-511-8656 / 512-245-2322
www.txstate.edu

Founded	1954 (Catalog: 2007-2008)
Accreditation	Southern Association of Colleges & Schools
External Degree	None
Tuition	$211.00
Text Cost	Not Listed / Full bibliography
Time Limits	Maximum 9 months / Minimum 45 days / 3-month extension @ $35.00
Transfer Hours	Non-Applicable
Curriculum	Topics in Mathematics for the Secondary Teacher 3-0 (1)
Comments	GOOD tuition rates. Good catalog. Incarcerated students.

University of Arizona
Independent Study through Correspondence
Office of Continuing Education & Outreach

P.O. Box 210158, Tucson AZ 85721-0158
800-772-7480 / 520-626-5667
www.arizona.edu

Founded	1915 (Catalog: 2007-2008)
Accreditation	North Central Association of Colleges & Schools UCEA
External Degree	None
Tuition	$290.00 / $15.00 per course fee (ER: 295.00)
Text Cost	Listed (new & used) / Full bibliography
Time Limits	Maximum 9 months / 3-month extension @ $40.00 fee
Transfer Hours	Non-Applicable
Curriculum	Agricultural Education (1 course) Family Studies & Human Development (1 course) Geosciences (1 course) Special Education, Rehabilitation & School Psychology (1 course)
Comments	AVERAGE tuition rates. Good catalog. Incarcerated students.

University of Central Arkansas
Division of Academic Outreach
Extended Study Program

Brewer-Hegeman Conference Center, Suite 102
201 Donaghey Avenue, Conway AR 72035
501-450-3118
www.uca.edu/aoep

Founded	1920 (2007-2008)
Accreditation	North Central Association of Colleges & Schools
External Degree	None
Tuition	$201.00 per credit + $38.50 in total fees per hour (ER: $239.50)
Text Cost	Not Listed / No bibliography listed
Time Limits	Maximum 6 months / 6-month extension @ $120.00
Transfer Hours	Non-Applicable
Curriculum	Education Statistics
Comments	AVERAGE tuition rates. Good Catalog.

University of Georgia
Center for Continuing Education

1197 South Lumpkin Street Suite 193, Athens GA 30602-3603
800-877-3243 / 706-542-3243
www.uga.edu

Founded	Unknown (Catalog 2007-2008)
Accreditation	Southern Association of Colleges & Schools
External Degree	None
Tuition	$171.00 (ER: $171.00)
Text Cost	Not Listed
Time Limits	Maximum 9 months / 3-month extension @ $60.00 fee
Transfer Hours	Non-Applicable
Curriculum	Accounting – Taxation I (ACCT 5400) Health – Effects of Drug Use & Abuse (HPRB 5210)
Comments	GOOD tuition rates. Good catalog; has section regarding prisoner enrollment (page 6). Incarcerated students.

University of Kansas
Independent Study

1515 St. Andrews Drive, Lawrence KS 66047
877-404-5823 / 785-864-7894
www.ku.edu

Founded	1891 (Catalog: 2007-2008)
Accreditation	North Central Association of Colleges & Schools
External Degree	None
Tuition	$285.65 per credit hour / $50.00 per course fee (ER: $302.98)
Text Cost	Not Listed / Per course materials cost listed
Time Limits	Maximum 9 months / 3-month extension @ $40.00 fee
Transfer Hours	Non-Applicable
Curriculum	Applied Behavioral Sciences (1) Psychology (2) Curriculum & Teaching (1) Educational Leadership & Policy Studies (1) Special Education (1)
Comments	AVERAGE tuition rates. Good catalog. Incarcerated students enrolled.

University of Missouri
Center for Distance Education & Independent Study

136 Clark Hall, Columbia MO 65211-4200
800-699-3727 / 573-882-2491
www.missouri.edu

Founded	1911 (Catalog: 2007-2008)
Accreditation	North Central Association of Colleges & Schools AACIS
External Degree	None
Tuition	$286.90 per credit / $11.70 per credit fee (ER: $298.60)
Text Cost	Listed with full bibliography
Time Limits	Maximum 9 months/ 3-month extension @ $35.00 fee
Transfer Hours	Non-Applicable
Curriculum	Issues & Trends in Reading Instruction (3 credits) The Secondary School Curriculum (3 credits) Administration of Programs for Children & Families (3 credits)
Comments	AVERAGE tuition rates. Good catalog.

NOTE: By taking courses from this school you will be supporting a bloated penal system. The Missouri state legislature has financed the eighth largest per capita incarceration rate by proportionally decreasing allocations from the higher education budget (necessitating inflated tuitions) and shifting funding to the penal system. Therefore, every time someone pays tuition, they are inadvertently supporting the incarceration of a prisoner. It's your choice, but there are other options to choose from. Make an economic-ethical-political statement by boycotting this school.

University of Northern Iowa
Guided Independent Study

2637 Hudson Road, Cedar Falls IA 50614-0223
800-772-1746 / 319-273-2123
www.uni.edu

Founded	Unknown (2007-2008)
Accreditation	North Central Association of Colleges & Schools
External Degree	
Tuition	$174.00 per credit hour & $13.00 per course fee (ER: $179.33)
Text Cost	Not Listed / No Bibliography
Time Limits	Minimum 6 weeks / Maximum 9 months / 3-month extension @ $15.00
Transfer Hours	Non-Applicable
Curriculum	Communications (1 course) Design, Textiles, Gerontology & Family Studies (1) Education – Elementary & Middle Level Education (2) Physical Education (1) Social Foundations (1) Psychology (2)
Requirements	Marketing (1) Religion (1) Social Work (2) Sociology & Criminology (5)
Comments	EXCELLENT tuition rates. Good catalog. Incarcerated students.

Index

High School Programs

ALPHABETICAL
American School
Brigham Young University
Continental Academy
Griggs International University
Hadley School for the Blind
Indiana University
Keystone National High School
North Dakota Center for Distance Education
Portland State University
Stratford Career Institute
Texas Tech University
University of Alabama
University of Arizona
University of Idaho
University of Missouri
University of Nebraska - Lincoln
University of Nevada – Reno
University of Oklahoma
University of Wisconsin

DIPLOMA PROGRAMS
American School
Brigham Young University
Continental Academy
Griggs International University
Hadley School for the Blind
Indiana University
North Dakota Center for Distance Education
Stratford Career Institute
Texas Tech University
University of Missouri
University of Nebraska – Lincoln
University of Oklahoma

BEST TUITION BUYS
American School
Brigham Young University
Continental Academy
Hadley School for the Blind
North Dakota Center for Distance Education
University of Idaho

Vocational Programs

ALPHABETICAL
Adams State College (2)
American Bible Academy
American Institute of Applied Sciences (2)
Catholic Distance University
Cleveland Institute of Electronics (13)
Cornell Lab of Ornithology
Global University
Graduate School, USDA
Moody Bible Institute
National Tax Training School (2)
Rhodec International (2)
Seminary Extension
SJM Family Foundation, Inc.
Stratford Career Institute (7)
The Hadley School for the blind (3)
University of Arizona
University of Georgia (3)
University of Wisconsin

Vocational Programs Areas of Study

BROADCAST ENGINEERING
Cleveland Institute of Electronics

COMPUTER TECHNOLOGY
Cleveland Institute of Electronics (2)

COMPUTER PROGRAMMING
Cleveland Institute of Electronics (2)

DISASTER MANAGEMENT
University of Wisconsin

DISPUTE RESOLUTION
Adams State College
University of Wisconsin

ELECTRONICS
Cleveland Institute of Electronics (6)

FORENSIC SCIENCE
American Institute of Applied Science (2)

INTERIOR DESIGN
Rhodec International

MANAGEMENT
Graduate School, USDA

MEDICAL BILLING SPECIALIST
Stratford Career Institute

ORNITHOLOGY
Cornell Lab of Ornithology

RELIGIOUS INSTRUCTION
American Bible Academy
Catholic Distance University
Global University
Moody Bible Institute
Seminary Extension

TAX PREPARATION
National Tax Training School

TURFGRASS MANAGEMENT
University of Georgia

Paralegal Programs

Adams State College
  Legal Investigation Certificate
Adams State College
  Paralegal Certificate Course
Ashworth University
  Associate Degree Paralegal Studies
American Center
  for Conflict Resolution Institute
  Paralegal / Legal Assistant
American Center
  for Conflict Resolution Institute.
  Professional Business & Family Mediator
Blackstone Career Institute
  Legal Assistant / Paralegal
Graduate School, USDA
  Paralegal Study Courses
Paralegal Institute
  Associate Degree
Paralegal Institute
  Criminal Justice Diploma
Paralegal Institute
  Legal Nurse Consultant
Paralegal Institute
  Paralegal Studies
Stratford Career Institute
  Legal Assistant / Paralegal
Newport University
  Juris Doctor

Undergraduate Colleges and Universities

Acadia University
Adams State College
Andrews University
Ashworth University
Brigham Young University
California Coast University
Catholic Distance University
Charter Oak State College
Cleveland Institute of Electronics (2)
Colorado State University – Pueblo
Columbia Union College
Global University
Governors State University
Graduate School, USDA
Huntington College of Health Science
Indiana University
Institute of Logistical Management
Lee University
Life Pacific College
Louisiana State University
Moody Bible Institute
Mountain State University
Newport University
Northern State University
Oakwood College
Ohio University
Oklahoma State University

Oral Roberts University
Portland State University
Sam Houston State College
Seminary Extension
Southwest University
Texas State University – San Marcos
Texas State University
Thomas Edison State College
University of Arizona
University of Arkansas
University of Central Arkansas
University of Colorado – Boulder
University of Georgia
University of Idaho
University of Illinois – Urban-Champaign
University of Kansas
University of Manitoba
University of Minnesota
University Of Mississippi
University of Missouri
University of Nebraska – Lincoln
University of Nevada – Reno
University of North Carolina
University of North Dakota
University of Northern Iowa
University of Saskatchewan
University of South Carolina
University of South Dakota
University of Utah
University of Wisconsin
University of Wisconsin – Plattesville
Upper Iowa University
Vincennes University
Western Washington University

Undergraduate Certificate Programs

ACCOUNTING
Graduate School, USDA
Indiana University

BIBLE / CHRISTIAN STUDIES
Global University
Life Pacific College
Moody Bible Institute
Seminary Extension

CATHETICAL DIPLOMA
Catholic Distance University

BUSINESS COMMUNICATION
Louisiana State University
Upper Iowa University

BUSINESS MANAGEMENT
Huntington College of Health Science

CRIMINAL JUSTICE / CRIMINOLOGY
Southwest University
University of Northern Iowa

EMERGENCY & DISASTER MANAGEMENT
Upper Iowa University

ENGLISH AS A SECOND LANGUAGE
University of Saskatchewan

FINANCIAL MANAGEMENT
Indiana University

HUMAN RESOURCE MANAGEMENT
Southwest University
University of Wisconsin – Plattesville
Upper Iowa University

HUMAN SERVICES
Louisiana State University

INTERNATIONAL BUSINESS
University of Wisconsin – Plattesville
Upper Iowa University

LIBERAL STUDIES
Louisiana State University

LOGISTICS
Institute of logistical Management

MANAGEMENT
Southwest University
University of Wisconsin – Plattesville
Upper Iowa University

METEOROLOGY
Graduate School, USDA

MINISTRY
Global University
Life Pacific College
Seminary Extension

NUTRITION
Huntington College of Health Science

THEOLOGY
Global University

Undergraduate Associate Degree Programs

ASSOCIATE OF ARTS
Adams State College
California Coast University
Charter Oak State College
Columbia Union College
Global University
Life Pacific College
Newport University
Thomas Edison State College
Upper Iowa University
Vincennes University

ASSOCIATE OF SCIENCES
Andrews University
Charter Oak State College
Columbia Union College
Southwest University
Thomas Edison State College
Vincennes University

ASSOCIATE DEGREES
Ashworth University
Huntington College of Health Sciences
Indiana University
Moody Bible Institute
Ohio University

ASSOCIATE OF APPLIED SCIENCES
Cleveland Institute of Electronics (2)
Ohio University
Vincennes University

Associate Degree Areas of Study

ACCOUNTING
Ashworth University

BUSINESS MANAGEMENT
Ashworth University
California Coast University
Columbia Union College
Ohio University
Southwest University
Thomas Edison State College
Upper Iowa University

COMPUTER INFORMATION MANAGEMENT
Ashworth University
Cleveland Institute of Electronics (2)

CONSTRUCTION MANAGEMENT
Ashworth University

CRIMINAL JUSTICE
Ashworth University

EDUCATION
Ashworth University

FINANCES
Ashworth University

GENERAL STUDIES
Andrews University
Indiana University
Thomas Edison State College
Upper Iowa University

HEALTHCARE
Ashworth University
Huntington College of Health Science

HUMAN RESOURCES
Ashworth University

MARKETING
Ashworth University

MINISTRIES
Andrews University
Global University
Life Pacific College

Psychology
Ashworth University
California Coast University
Columbia Union College

Religion
Global University
Moody Bible Institute

Security Management
Ashworth University

Social Services
Thomas Edison State College

Baccalaureate Programs

Bachelor of Arts
Adams University
Andrews University
Catholic Distance University
Charter Oak State college
Columbia Union College
Global Union
Newport University
Oakwood College
Oral Roberts University
Thomas Edison State College
University of Manitoba
University of North Dakota

Bachelor of Sciences
Adams State College
Andrews University
California Coast University
Charter Oak State College
Colorado State University – Pueblo
Columbia Union College
Huntington College of Health Science
Moody Bible Institute
Oral Roberts University
Southwest University
Thomas Edison State College
University of Wisconsin – Plattesville

Bachelor of General Studies
Indiana University

Ohio University
Texas Tech University
University of North Dakota
University of Northern Iowa

Baccalaureate Degree Majors & Minors

Accounting
University of Wisconsin – Plattesville

Business Administration
Adams State College
California Coast University
Columbia Union Collage
Newport University
Oral Roberts University
Southwest University
Thomas Edison State College
University of Wisconsin – Plattesville
California Coast University

Canadian Studies
University of Manitoba

Criminal Justice / Criminology
Colorado State University – Pueblo
Southwest University

Economics
University of Manitoba

English
University of Manitoba

General Studies
Columbia Union College
Indiana University
Oakwood College
Ohio University
Oral Roberts University
Texas Tech University

History
University of Manitoba

Humanities
Andrews University

Human Organization & Behavior
Andrews University
Newport University
Thomas Edison State College

Management
California Coast University

Ministries
Global University
Oral Roberts University

Political Science
University of Manitoba

Religion
Andrews University
Catholic Distance University
Columbia Union College
Global University
Moody Bible Institute
Oral Roberts University

Social Services
Colorado State University – Pueblo

Most (17) Majors & Minors
Upper Iowa University

Graduate Level Programs

Atlantic University
California Coast University
Catholic Distance university
Colorado State University
Global University
Huntington College of Health Science
Newport University
Southwest University
Texas State University – San Marcos
University of Arizona
University of Central Arkansas
University of Georgia
University of Kansas
University of Missouri
University of Northern Iowa

Graduate Certificates

Business Administration
Southwest University

Criminal Justice / Criminology
Southwest University
University of Northern Iowa

Catechism Of The Catholic Church And Catholic Bible
Catholic Distance University

Criminal Justice / Criminology
Southwest University
University of Northern Iowa

Leadership & Management
Southwest University
Catholic Distance University

Management
Southwest University

Organizational Management
Southwest University

Graduate Degree Programs

Business Administration
California Coast University
Newport University
Southwest University

Criminal Justice
Southwest University

Divinity
Global University

Education
California Coast University

Human Behavior
Newport University

Human Resource Management
California Coast University

Ministerial Studies
Global University

NUTRITION
Huntington College of Health Science

ORGANIZATIONAL MANAGEMENT
Southwest University

PSYCHOLOGY
California Coast University
Newport University

THEOLOGY
Catholic Distance University

TRANSPERSONAL STUDIES
Atlantic University

Doctoral Programs

HUMAN BEHAVIOR
Newport University

JURIS DOCTOR
Newport University

Earn an Adams State College Degree via Correspondence Courses

- Correspondence Courses via mail
- No internet access required
- Degree options available —
  Associate of Arts or Science
  Business Administration
  Interdisciplinary Studies
  Paralegal Certificate Program
- Affordable tuition — $125/semester hour for correspondence courses
- Accredited by the Higher Learning Commission of the North Central Association of Colleges and Schools
- Years of experience serving incarcerated students
- FREE unofficial evaluation of previously earned credits

Call or write to receive a free copy of our catalog
—800-548-6679
Office of Extended Studies, Box CC
Adams State College • 208 Edgemont Blvd. • Alamosa, CO 81102

ADAMS STATE COLLEGE
COLORADO
Great Stories Begin Here
EXTENDED STUDIES

exstudies.adams.edu

About Prison Legal News

PRISON LEGAL NEWS (PLN) is an independent, monthly magazine founded and edited by Paul Wright. Published since 1990, PLN is the longest-running independent, prisoner-produced magazine in U.S. history. With a national circulation of more than 7,000 subscribers, PLN focuses on reporting news and legal developments involving prisons, jails, and the criminal justice system. Each issue is packed with news, analysis, book reviews, and legal information. PLN's content is uncensored. PLN also distributes and publishes a wide variety of self help books relevant to prisoners and radical critiques of the criminal justice system.

PLN is a 501(c)(3) nonprofit and is almost entirely reader-supported. If you believe in the concept of an independent media that reports on prison and jail issues from a perspective other than that of the government, the private prison industry, or the "lock 'em up" crowd, subscribe to PLN today.

For more information about PLN, our back issues, and other related information, please go to PLN's Web site: WWW.PRISONLEGALNEWS.ORG. The staff of Prison Legal News thank you for reading this book. We hope your interest in this important topic does not end here. To continue receiving regular updates and articles about the U.S. prison system, prisoner struggle, human rights in American detention facilities, organizing, and legal and political developments found nowhere else, subscribe to Prison Legal News today.

Prison Legal News
2400 NW 80th St., PMB 148
Seattle WA 98117
(206) 781-6524
PLN@PRISONLEGALNEWS.ORG
WWW.PRISONLEGALNEWS.ORG

PRISON LEGAL NEWS
BRATTLEBORO, VERMONT • SEATTLE, WASHINGTON
Dedicated to Protecting Human Rights

THIRD EDITION

PRISONERS' GUERRILLA HANDBOOK

TO CORRESPONDENCE PROGRAMS IN THE UNITED STATES & CANADA

By **JON MARC TAYLOR**, PhD

Edited by Susan Schwartzkopf, MA

Foreword by Rev. Vivian Nixon

**HIGH SCHOOL • VOCATIONAL • PARALEGAL
LAW • COLLEGE • GRADUATE COURSES**

> "Copies of this very usable and useful guide should be available in every prison library—to help incarcerated people give positive direction to their energies while making constructive use of their time. It is a well-established fact that people who have taken college courses in prison have a dramatically reduced rate of recidivism."
>
> —BELL GALE CHEVIGNY, PEN PRISON WRITING PROGRAM, EDITOR *DOING TIME: 25 YEARS OF PRISON WRITING.*

HIGH SCHOOL • VOCATIONAL • PARALEGAL • UNDERGRADUATE • GRADUATE COURSES

THE GREATLY anticipated and newly updated third edition of the *Prisoner's Guerrilla Handbook to Correspondence Programs in the United States and Canada* has finally arrived! Author Jon Marc Taylor's brand new version is the latest in this unique and highly successful guidebook for the prisoner-student. This invaluable tool and **how-to handbook** provides the reader with **step-by-step instructions** to find the appropriate educational program for **high school, vocational, paralegal, undergraduate, and graduate courses** offered in the U.S. and Canada today.

Invaluable re-entry tool

It presents more than 160 program outlines and offers an **easy-to-use format** for the student to determine which program best suits their needs. It is ideal for the incarcerated student who does not have Internet access or the ability to attend education classes in person. This resource is indispensable for the individual and beneficial for use in all prison libraries and education departments.

The *Prisoner's Guerrilla Handbook* is the only book on the market for the non-traditional prisoner-student. It includes detailed listings of the quality, cost, and course offerings for all correspondence programs available to prisoners. In a time when so many academic opportunities in prisons have been eliminated, this book is an invaluable re-entry tool for prisoners who seek to further their education while incarcerated and to help them prepare for life and work following their release.

Jon Marc Taylor has more than 25 years experience as an incarcerated student, advocate for prisoner education, and author. He has successfully earned a bachelor's degree, a master's degree, and a doctorate via correspondence courses while incarcerated. Editor **Susan Schwartzkopf** has a master's degree in education and 12 years experience teaching immigrants English language skills.

PRISONERS' GUERRILLA HANDBOOK TO CORRESPONDENCE PROGRAMS IN THE UNITED STATES AND CANADA

By Jon Marc Taylor PhD

8.25" x 10.75" • 224 pages

ISBN 978-0-9819385-0-9

$49.95

3 or more copies ordered at once **$39.95** each

Number of copies ordered _____ Amount enclosed _____

By: ☐ check ☐ new postage stamps ☐ credit card ☐ money order

Name _____

DOC/BOP Number _____

Institution/Agency _____

PUBLISHED BY

PRISON LEGAL NEWS
Dedicated to Protecting Human Rights

2400 N. W. 80th Street #148 • Seattle WA 98117
Tel [206] 246-1022 • www.prisonlegalnews.org